Los Indignados: Tides of Social Insertion in Spain

Los Indignados: Tides of Social Insertion in Spain

Richard R. Weiner and Iván López

Winchester, UK
Washington, USA

First published by Zero Books, 2018
Zero Books is an imprint of John Hunt Publishing Ltd., Laurel House, Station Approach,
Alresford, Hants, SO24 9JH, UK
office1@jhpbooks.net
www.johnhuntpublishing.com
www.zero-books.net

For distributor details and how to order please visit the 'Ordering' section on our website.

Text copyright: Richard R. Weiner and Iván López 2017

ISBN: 978 1 78535 312 3
978 1 78535 313 0 (ebook)
Library of Congress Control Number: 2016945822

A CIP catalogue record for this book is available from the British Library.

Design: Stuart Davies

Cover image: "Íñigo Errejón of the Podemos bloc makes a point in the Spanish parliament."
Albert DiLolli, El Mundo, 13 January 2016

Printed and bound by CPI Group (UK) Ltd, Croydon, CR0 4YY, UK

We operate a distinctive and ethical publishing philosophy in
all areas of our business, from our global network of authors to
production and worldwide distribution.

26-J elections Unidos Podemos electoral poster
Source: Unidos Podemos

Contents

For our sons Gael, Aimar, Sean and Yann and
their futures

Introduction and Acknowledgments

The Spanish Cockpit is the title of Franz Borkenau's 1937 book on the flows, the entanglements, and the enfolding/unfolding of the Spanish Revolution for democracy and the Counter-Revolution led by General Francisco Franco. Spain today is again a cockpit – amidst legitimation crises; amidst the precarity engendered by over three decades of neoliberal political economy; and amidst the extension of a transition to democracy. Ironically, a movement for democratizing has emerged in the celebrated post-Franco consolidation of liberal democracy.

Our short book traces the commitment, the élan, and the vision of *Los Indignados* as a movement of practices and claims for a further Transition on the Spanish road to democracy – a movement called from the future, breaking with the past.

Following Alain Touraine's sociology of social movement as an institutionalizing leveraging to reorganize the *field of historicity*, the authors have been keeping up with Los Indignados for these past four years. This movement of "the Enraged" (Indignants) starts in both the 15-M (15 May 2011) occupation of the Puerta del Sol in Madrid and an anti-evictions movement in Catalonia in the wake of the 2008 Great Recession.

We sensed that Los Indignados was a movement redefining practices within a struggle of grassroots *municipalismo*. These tended to be a decentered and non-totalizing movement for interurban and interregional social pacts, as well as a "plurinational" reframing of the Spanish peoples. Eventually, in 2014, an electorally oriented political arm emerged to coordinate these tides for reinserting/re-embedding a notion of social sustainability for the twenty-first century.

These critical citizens' practices reveal a genealogy of moral revaluation as reciprocal solidarity of a more sharing economy. A most overused buzzword of the new century is "resilience":

1

understood as our bouncing back from turbulence, vulnerability, disaster. Somehow the concept of solidarity has been eclipsed, defined minimally as a synonym for the downward-flowing social protection of the state. Social solidarity can be better understood as a resilience bubbling up from below in a new form of social "pact-ing" of *Homo reciprocans* rather than *Homo economicus* (see Bowles and Gintis, 1998). This is a form of social pacting that is neither opaque nor exclusive, one not imbricated within a cartelized or corporatist membrane reminiscent of Franco's Vertical Syndicate, and not sustained in what Juan Linz refers to as the post-Franco minimalist Transition toward democratization. This had been a pacting by a political class (*La Casta*) of bipartisan political parties (PP, PSOE). The minimalist Transition – obsessed with consensus and forgetting the trauma of the Civil War – has been only a surface dismantling of the Vertical Syndicate, making use of direct government grants to co-opt the trade union movement.

This short book genealogically studies this emerging new phenomenon of bonding connection as a significant new social form and framework of knowledge, creating critical space for institutionalizing leverage. The New Transition recalls Spanish traditions of municipal mutual aid initiatives (1840s–1936) within a confluence strategy of municipalist, interurban, and interregional pacts among the Popular Unity platforms and "Tides" (*mareas*) associated with the evolving 15-M Indignados movement. The book makes a start at identifying a promising new form of social pacting among what Elinor Ostrom (1990) categorizes as reciprocators (*reciproqueteurs*), not atomized and isolated entrepreneurs (cf. Ostrom and Walker, 2009).

The book serves both as a political sociology argument and as a sourcebook with an introductory timeline to grasp genealogy, and with an introductory overview of the most significant of the more than 1,000 political parties in 52 Spanish provinces – what Indignados leaders Ada Colau and Juan Carlos Monedero wryly refer to as a "soup of acronyms."

We have discussed many of the arguments in papers presented at annual conferences of the Conference of Europeanists based at Columbia University, World Congresses of the International Political Science Association, as well as at the University of Chicago, the University of Vienna, and the New York City Telos Conferences. Our ruminations draw upon the continuing stimulation of seminars for over two decades at the Minda de Gunzburg Center for European Studies at Harvard University. Special note must be made of the inspiring examples in guiding urban movements by Henry Shelton and Carol Shelton of the George Wiley Center in Providence and Frances Fox Piven in New York City.

We have been bolstered by the encouragement of Ramón Cotarelo, Universidad Nacional de Educación a Distancia, Madrid; Juan Díez Medrano, Universidad Carlos III, Madrid; and Miguel Ángel Ruiz de Azua, Universidad Complutense, Madrid; as well as the many kindnesses and guidance provided by Alain Touraine over the decades starting with his Centre d'étude des mouvements sociaux, EHESS, Paris. A word of thanks to online journals that have provided up-to-the-minute reporting on the unfolding genealogy of Los Indignados: *Open Democracy*, *Left Flank*, and *Jacobin*. For Andrew Buchwalter, Thomas Cobb, William Hutchinson, Edward Markward, Laurence Marlow, Mark Motte, and Irvin Schonfeld, a special note of gratefulness for the sustenance and understanding that enduring friendship brings. For Amy Tibbetts at Rhode Island College and Helen Pardoe at John Hunt Publishing a bouquet of appreciation for help in editing and merging files. Many thanks to Yann Weiner in assuring high resolution of pictures and figures in a digitizing century. And to our patient partners Danielle and Brenda, the biggest thanks of all.

Providence and Zaragoza

Spanish Political Parties
("a soup of acronyms")

Right

JONS   Falange Española de las JONS/Juntas des Ofensiva Nacional Sindicalists (Falangist Party) – last contested elections 2004

PP   Partido Popular (Popular Party) – 123 out of 350 Congress seats, 20 December 2015 national elections

Nationalist Right

CiU   Convergencia/Unió (Catalan Convergence and Union Party)

EAJ/PNV   Euzko Alderdi Jeltzalea/Partido Nacionalista Vasco (Basque Nationalist Party) – 9 Congress seats, 20 December 2015

CC   BNG should end with 7/75 "regional parliament"... See RW6 above – 1 Congress seat, 20 December 2015

DiL   Democràcia i Llibertat (Catalan Democracy and Freedom) – 8 out of 350 Congress seats, 20 December 2015

FAC   Foro Asturias (Asturian Forum) – 8/45 regional parliament

PA   Partido Aragonés (Aragonese Party) – 6/67 regional parliament

UPN   Unión del Pueblo Navarro (Navarese People's Union) – 15/50 regional parliament

Nationalist Center

Junts per Si   Together for Yes!/Catalan Independence Party – 62/135 regional parliament

4

PRC	Partido Regionalista de Cantabria – 12/35 regional parliament

Center Right

C's	Ciudadanos (Citizens/Party of the Citizenry) – 40 Congress seats, 20 December 2015
UPyD	Partido Unión, Progreso y Democracia (Union, Progress and Democracy Party) – 0 Congress seats, 20 December 2015

Center Left

PSOE	Partido Socialista Obrero Español (Socialist Workers Party), affiliated with labor confederation UGT (Unión General de Trabajadores – General Workers' Union) – 90 out of 350 Congress seats, 20 December 2015
PDNI	Partido Democrática de la Nueva Izquierda (Party of the Democratic Left), aligned with PSOE
GBai	Geroa Bai (Yes to the Future Party) (Basque) – 9/50 regional parliament

Nationalist Left

AGE/Anova	Alternative Galega de Esquerda (Galician Alternative of the Left) – 6/75 regional parliament
Amaiur	Amaiur/Ezker Abertzala (Basque Nationalist Party)
BNG	Bloque Nacionalista Galego 7/75 (regional and national parliament)
Catalonia Sí que es Pot!/En Comú Podem	Catalonia Yes We Can! Modeled after Barcelona en Comú. Composed of Podemos, ICV: Initiative for Catalonia Greens, and EUiA: United Alternative – 11/135 regional parliament
CHC	Chunta Aragonesista (Aragonese Union)
Compromís	Coalició Compromís (Valencia Commitment

	Coalition), aligned with Podemos – 1 Congress seat, 20 December 2015 national elections and 4/33 regional parliament
CUP	Candidatura d'Unitat Popular (Popular Unity Candidacy for Catalonia) – 10/135 regional parliament
ERC	Esquerra Republicana de Catalunya (Republican Left of Catalonia)
ICV	Iniciativa per Catalunya Verds (Initiative for Catalan Greens)
I-E	Izquierd-Eskerra/Plataforma Navarra por el Cambio – S2/50 regional parliament
IzAb	Izquierda Abierta Madrid/Open Left (Gaspar Llamarzes) within Izquierda Unida de Asturias

Left

AeC	Ahora en Común/Confluence (Now in Common/ Confluence), renamed Unidad Popular (Popular Unity) – 2 out of 350 Congress seats, 20 December 2015
(A)	Anarkosindikalismoa (Anarchosyndicalists), affiliated with the syndicalist-oriented CNT (Confederación Nacional Trabajo)
eQuo	Equo/Confederation of 30 Spanish Green Parties, aligned with Podemos – 3 out of 350 Congress seats, 20 December 2015
IU	Izquierda Unida (United Left), successor to PCE/Plural Left – 2 out of 350 Congress seats, 20 December 2015 (Izquierda Anticapitalista, formerly Espacio Alternativo).
PCE	Partido Communista de España (former Spanish Communist Party), affiliated with CC.OO. (Confederación Sindical de Comisiones Obreros – Workers' Commissions)

PCE (r)   Partido Communista de España (Reconstituido) (Spanish Communist Party Reconstituted)

(P)   Podemos (Yes We Can!/Circles), aligned with En Comú Podem – 69 out of 350 Congress seats, 20 December 2015 (41 purely Podemos)

1

Encountering Eruption: Tides of Social Insertion

The writing on the wall: *"No hay pan para tanto chorizo."*
(There is not enough bread for so much pork.)

Spain has witnessed in the wake of the economic crisis of 2008 what Henri Lefebvre would call an "eruption" of liminal spaces of possibility, new spaces of social insertion, new spaces of self-spreading flows of new elective affinities. These are spaces of a new becoming. First, there is disaffection from the political class and financial elites complicit in the post-Franco Transition State constituted by the Moncloa Pacts of October 1977. Second, there are rights claims that characterize a new sense of the "social" (cf. Donzelot, 1984; Castoriadis, 1978; Castel, 1995): a sense resisting the statist rhetoric of social protection and the "social washing" of professional spin masters.

The authors first met in Madrid in the summer of 2012, sharing in the 15-M movement occupying the Puerta del Sol as well as other central plazas in other major Spanish cities, and finding remarkable Ada Colau's anti-evictions movement in Catalonia. Since then, we have been daily witnessing and studying the unfolding of a movement redefining practices within a struggle of grassroots municipalism. A moving – as Colau notes – from "occupy to planning democracy in Spain." That movement is decentered and non-totalizing in the resilience of its interurban and interregional social "pact-ing," and its plurinational reframing of the Spanish peoples.

For the 15-M movement and the PAH: *Plataforma de Afectados por la Hipoteca* (Platform for People Affected by Mortgages), there is a perceived manifest decline in trust in the politicians of the Transition State as well as in the financial services industry, turned to for triggering a mirage of sustainable economic growth. Spurred by Stéphane Hessel's 2010 pamphlet-style call to action, *Indignez-vous!*, this is the outrage of a lost generation. They are *Los Indignados*: cut off and massively unemployed youth – cut off from the circuits of capital accumulation, workplace habitus, and the pillars of social democracy. The outraged grandchildren of the Spanish welfare state confront the complicity in, and culpability for, the austerity policies provoked by the bursting of the 1992–2007 credit bubble economy, itself generated by the investment algorithms of financial market actors and credit rating agencies.

The Outraged represent alternative experienced forms of life within what Gilles Deleuze refers to as horizontal and rhizomatic networks. Therein these new spaces are fugitive flashes of a prefigurative reciprocal solidarity – apart from Emile Durkheim's functionally differentiated organic solidarity. These flashes are glimmers of a fugitive intersubjectivity taking control of possibility, rather than some totalizing remaking of society.

The Indignados recall André Gorz's meditation on 1968: *Farewell to the Working Class*. They are the actualization of Gorz's prescient sensing of a coming precarious non-class in a farewell to the middle class.

The Transition State was not a revolutionary break with the past, but a further evolution of Francoism through a series of negotiated pacts acknowledging and warranting the rights of opposition. After Franco, Adolfo Suárez – in guiding the Moncloa Pacts – sought an increased pluralism with a restricted state. This was actually concertation rather than statist corporatism of the Catholic chambers legacy. These were not "social pacts" but political pacts involving political party elites consulting with their constituents in emergent so-called civil society associations (Pérez-Diaz, 1993). Yet Suárez sought to eliminate Marxists from the economic ministries, and business elites. He resisted the possibility of the state executing any form of socialist economic program (Encarnación, 1997: 409). For critics like Ramón Cotarelo et al. (2015: 167-71, 176) and Juan Carlos Monedero (2011), these were not pacts to rupture with the past, but a recursive return to a path along *el Camino Real*, a veritable Bourbon Restoration, if not its persistence. Such a new fashioning of a persistent form was accepted so long as benefits were capable of being provided to so many.

A consolidation of the young Spanish democracy seemed achieved with the victories of the Socialist Workers Party (PSOE) under Felipe González, first in October 1982, followed by wins in 1986, 1989, and 1993, and accession to the European Economic Community, soon to be renamed the European Union (EU). However, González would mine the cult of personality (*personalismo*), a staple of Spanish political culture. And *Felipismo* became easily entangled in the recurrent paths of corrupt cronyism of regime-supporting family networks. By 1987–8, hope for a more German social partnership form of concertation (see Lehmbruch, 1998) – of a state with civil society associations – broke down as González's PSOE-led government divorced itself from the UGT (Unión General del Trabajo) and its call for a general strike (Encarnación, 1997: 413).

Like Gerhard Schroeder's SPD in Germany and Blair's New Labour in Britain, González's PSOE adapted to the embeddedness of neoliberalism in the global political economy. In the three years after 2008 – the last three years of the government of the next PSOE prime minister, José Luis Rodríguez Zapatero – there were difficulties in evoking a sense of institutional trust. Zapatero and his government's austerity policies would be seen as responding less to the social rights achievements of his party, and more to the demands and interests of transnational economic actors, and especially the *Troika* of the International Monetary Fund (IMF) and both the European Commission and European Central Bank (ECB) within the EU.

Cascading legitimation crises buffeted Spain: the crisis of stagnant wages of the middle class; the crisis of rapidly expanding inequality; the crisis in sustaining the welfare state; the crisis of continued low economic growth; the crisis of the decline in labor unions' power and capability; the failure of the education system to adapt to technology and market needs; and the crisis of the Transition State's credibility itself. The discredited Transition State's difficulty in evoking institutional trust had become a significant causal factor.

What has been revealed is a strategy of *Confluence* of disaffection, legitimation claims, and collective identity. Los Indignados is not some prefigurative moment or early stage in the coming of a political party called *Podemos* (Yes We Can!). It is a movement of municipalist and interurban platforms and cooperative projects that become aligned with an anti-eviction movement, and a movement of over 50% youth unemployment (the *Precariat*).

What is constituted discursively is what Charles Tilly (2008) calls a *trust regime* wherein there is an imaginary framework with which to reconfigure institutional practices. This Confluence can be understood as a social ontology of what William Connolly (1987: 157–60) refers to as articulated "discordances in the unities we seek." This antagonistic discordance is discerned as a feeling of righteous breaking-off and provocative counterpoint to the referents, rhythms, and resonance of the post-Franco Transition State. The Confluence is a diffuse and multiscalar reconfiguring of spaces with transversal negotiations and projections. It can be understood as the Plural Social Subjects of Rights, rather than the time-honored Marxist Social Subjects of Rights, bearers of rights claims rather than bearers of structural forces and supports. The Confluence involves a social pacting from the bottom up. It swells, overflows, and displaces the limits of the Transition State. The social pacting among the diverse movements is a complementary institutionalizing – not just some overlapping consensus. Mutual emancipatory purposes are pursued in a reinforcing and sustaining manner.

The Indignados movement of Confluence against a perceived unrepresentative and unresponsive Transition State amounts to more than effervescence. It is the conflating – bringing together – of the legitimation claims of Social Subjects of Rights: on the one hand, contesting and intent on remaking the field of power relations; and on the other, manifesting an unfolding emergent intersubjectivity of mutual assistance. There is a reciprocal willingness to share in the responsibility of adapting to, pooling, and managing risk and vulnerability. Flesher-Fominaya (2015a, 2015b, 2015c) notes that the tides of social insertion – for example, in Madrid, Barcelona, Galicia, Valencia, and Aragon – make possible new types of credit pools and mutual enterprises.

The movement for a socially pacted democracy in Spain is a broad signifier foreshadowing a more confederal frame of thinking which can imaginatively anticipate and project a more flexible institutional architecture for a polycentric and plurinational Spain. It is one where citizens weave themselves together into a confederated cooperative meshwork wherein legitimation claims/rights claims can be leveraged for bargaining, as Frances Fox Piven (1977, 2008) reminds us. It is an unfolding/ enfolding revaluation of meanings and commitments, initiating and opening up learning spaces, and even evolving into a permanent institutionalizing presence; a movement in reaction to perceived social looting that first builds connections, then elective affinities and popular assemblies, and then mutually organized alternatives.

This is a resilient movement of mutual assistance grounded in a new form of social pacting, no longer imbricated in either a cartelized Franquist husk or a social partnership subverted by González's accommodations with neoliberalism. It amounts to a co-production and insertion of the social as a mutually referential network of mutual assistance, autonomous interdependencies, and social media platforms – what the Indignados refer to as the "Tides of Social Insertion." These are interlinked movements grounded in a new kind of pacting, a hybridized one that is more horizontally constituted and transversally negotiated across the scales, resisting the *assujetissement* (subjectification) of neoliberal dispositions and frames of thinking. Beyond resisting, theirs is an effort to scale up the sharing of local initiatives of social assertion and social insertion.

Social insertion is understood as a new form and as a new space:

- It is understood as *an embodied form of knowledge, and as a new mediated form of politics*: an ensemble of new interpretive frames embedded and lodged both alongside and within a new Transition State. Thus, Indignados is a movement constituted by its own asserted and inserted social frameworks of knowledge and their signifying meaning.

- It is also understood as *a new social space of possibility*: a space of flows, a new moral economy, a new political ecology of social praxis. This is an imaginatively created symbolic space for posing and trying alternative forms of life: new discursive opportunities, new manners of speaking, new participation codes, and, most importantly, new trust networks (Flesher-Fominaya, ibid.). Trust-producing resources provide the "glue" Peter Marcuse (2011) sees as vital in holding together the Movement for Social Insertion: resources that are regenerated as bonds, as shared values and norms, and as realized new capabilities.

In leveraging and scaling up movement initiatives and mobilization, the Indignados made use of social media online platforms – engaging in what is becoming known as "platform politics" in the trust network they had been building for the "horizontal democracy" (*horizontalidad*) they proclaimed. These complemented institutionally the movement's horizontalist/ heterarchical assemblies of deliberative democracy – or "circles" (*circulos*) as Podemos would call them and make part of their brand. Interface was now digitally intersubjective as well as eye-to-eye discursively intersubjective. This was especially so in the early years of PAH and the *municipalismo* revival.

Digital interface between laptops, smartphone devices, and their programs became a new point of conjuncture, and an expansion of spatial capability and autonomy in the development and dispersion of prefigurative movement conceptions, designs, rallies, and occupations. This amounts to spatial reorganization – in varieties of "parallel spaces": the development of new alternative infrastructures of political communication and the production of social learning. Network nodes were not centrally coordinated; they were becoming increasingly decentered/ decentralized. Trust networking – increasingly called "paranodality" – involves more than a single dominating code.

This is the making use of a new disposition to blog contentiously: asserting legitimation in rights claims; redrawing space and boundaries; renegotiating relations with the state. Blogging diarists become activists to persuade co-producers of the social reassertion/insertion in mutually referent networks. Confluence of tides is grounded in digitally empowered public space where sustainable community-based organizations are devised and put into effect with a more socialist than capitalist sense of a shared economy – a sensibility grounded in solidarity-based exchanges and networks. Economists in the Society for the Advancement of Socio-Economics (SASE) have come to brand this new form as *sustainable community movement organizations* (SCMOs).

2

Timeline of Tides of Social Insertion and Confluence

February 2009 – In Barcelona, Ada Colau helps form *Plataforma de Afectados por la Hipoteca* (Platform for People Affected by Mortgages) with a "Stop Evictions" campaign which spreads to 150 branches throughout Spain. By the autumn of 2014 this movement has prevented 1135 evictions in Spain and evolves into a more encompassing assembly-based citizens' platform entitled *Guanyem Barcelona* (Let's Win Back Barcelona), and in the spring 2015 municipal elections as *Barcelona en Comú* (Barcelona in Common) as a "Popular Unity" electoral coalition.

January 2011 – In the wake of the sweeping overhaul of labor market rules by Rodríguez Zapatero's government, designed to reduce unemployment and revive the economy by flexing up labor law, a call goes out from the syndicalist labor confederation UGT and the communist CCOO. for the first general strike in a decade. Mass demonstrations break out in Madrid, Galicia, Catalonia, and the Basque country.

February 2011 – Users of social networks create digital citizens' platform *Democracia Real YA!* (Real Democracy Now!) to resist Rodríguez Zapatero's PSOE-based government's attempt (*La Ley Sinde*) to shut down web pages with links or downloads from copyrighted material.

15 May 2011 – Hundreds of thousands of citizens take to the plazas of Spain's cities to protest against cutbacks in the welfare state imposed by the Troika of the International Monetary Fund, the European Commission of the EU, and the European

Central Bank of the EU, and implemented like an intendent by the ostensibly social democratic government of Prime Minister Rodríguez Zapatero. They then begin to camp out in the squares in settlements, called *acampadas*, staying on and on. A movement called 15-M quickly spreads through social media/information and communication technologies (ICTs) being used as crucial instruments of political deliberation and coordination. By the end of 2011 upwards of 7 to 8 million participate in the protests.

21 May 2011 – Throughout the occupied plazas, demonstrators perform the "Mute Scream" of protest followed by cheers and applause.

20–25 May 2011 – Indignant People's March begins throughout Spain, heeding the call to walk to Madrid and meet at the Puerta del Sol. Polls show 70% of Spaniards support the demonstrations and marches.

27 May 2011 – The Barcelona City Council attempts to clear the Plaça de Catalunya for the Champions League title football match between FC Barcelona and Manchester United.

23 July 2011 – Indignant People's March reaches Madrid and converges in eight columns, collapsing entrances into Madrid where they are joined by sympathizers. Their experiences are recorded in "The Book of the People."

17 September 2011 – "We are the 99%" slogan emerges.

3 October 2011 – "Occupy Together" website emerges along with "Occupy Our Homes," "Occupy Our Freedoms," and "Occupy Our Mines."

20 November 2011 – The conservative Partido Popular (PP) wins the general elections, achieving an absolute majority. A good part of the population still dreams of the glorious years of spectacular economic growth from José María Aznar's conservative government (1996–2004: "the economic miracle"). The incoming government approves 20 decrees over the first six months and 29 in 2012 (more than any other government in democracy).

April 2012 – The European Court of Justice in Luxemburg rules that Spanish mortgage laws contravened EU directive.

May 2012 – Asturias coal miners demonstrate, begin industrial action, and march on Madrid. First anniversary of the 15 May occupations.

2012–13 – The *Mareas* (Tides of Change) demonstrations on matters beyond wage issues, organized by citizen assemblies and platforms: *marea blanca* (white tide) against government health services cutbacks; *marea verde* (green tide) of elementary and secondary school teachers; *marea roja* (red tide) focusing on the unemployed; *marea violeta* (violet tide) against sexist violence and the the recently approved most restrictive European Union law on abortion; and *marea azul* (blue tide) against privatization of water. Brought together as *Marea Ciudadana* (Citizens' Tides) in a coalition of 350 organizations – from health groups to trade unions to youth groups – mobilizing hundreds of thousands against policies of privatization and austerity, Citizens' Tides pushes for an audit of Spain's national debt under the slogan "We don't owe. We won't pay."

16 January 2014 – *Podemos* (Yes We Can!), a political party, is founded, dedicated to the commitments and objectives of the Indignados movement. Its major leaders and manifesto signees include Pablo Iglesias, Juan Carlos Monedero, Iñigo Errejón,

Carolina Bescansa and Teresa Rodríguez. Many are political science and law professors from the Complutense University of Madrid. Monedero and Errejón have worked with the Pink Tides of revived socialism in Latin America. Iglesias completed a PhD dissertation on the anti-globalization movement emerging at the World Trade Organization summit in Seattle in 1999.

22 March 2014 – *Marcha por Dignidad* (March for Dignity) – an anti-austerity demonstration soon to be called M-22 – demanding "no more cuts" and including many 30-year-olds as well as 60- and 70-year-olds swarms the Puerta del Sol with close to 200,000 marchers.

18 May 2014 – A film about Spain's lost generation of unemployed youth, *Hermosa Juventud* (Beautiful Youth), directed by the acclaimed Jaime Rosales, premiers at the Cannes Festival and is awarded Ecumenical Jury Special Mention.

25 May 2014 – Five Podemos Members of the European Parliament are elected and nets 8% of the national vote.

14 July 2014 – *CIS* quarterly survey shows Podemos surpassing PSOE as the second most popular political party in Spain.

2 November 2014 – *El Pais* poll puts Podemos in first place in approval ratings with 27.7%, over 26.2% for PSOE, and 20.7% for the ruling Popular Party. 22.2% indicate a "direct intention to vote" the same way, double the percentage for each of the other parties.

15 September – 15 November 2014 – Podemos holds a month-long Citizens' Congress to determine party policy and resolutions to adopt. The Congress brought together representatives in person and online from grassroots assemblies called "circles" that had blossomed all over Spain since the 2008 financial crisis and the 15 May 2011 occupations. Podemos decides not to stand directly in the March and May 2015 municipal and regional elections, and instead to support local grassroots candidates from Popular Unity platforms such as *Ahora Madrid* (Now Madrid) and *Barcelona en Comú* (Barcelona in Common). Policy positions included restructuring Spain's government debt of 1 trillion euros; tighter corporate regulation; a universal basic income; and opposition to the Transatlantic Trade and Investment Pact between the EU and USA on the grounds that the pact threatens labor shares and will create job losses, while making it even harder for individual governments to regulate transnational corporations which would be subject to investor/state displacement requiring settlement arbitration beyond borders. It was decided to set up a Committee of Guarantees to guard procedures and protocols, and a 62-person Citizens' Council. A contest between the two contending platforms for leadership of Podemos emerged. *Sumando Podemos* (Summing Up We Can), led by recently elected MEPs Teresa Rodríguez, Pablo Echenique, and Lola Sánchez, argued for a collective leadership. *Claro Que Podemos* (Of Course We Can), led by Pablo Iglesias, Iñigo Errejón, Juan Carlos Monedero, and Carolina Bescansa, argued for a single general secretary with a supporting team elected as a whole, a Citizens' Council composed of 87 members. Claro Que Podemos wins with 80.9 %, compared to *Sumando Podemos* with 12.3 %. Iglesias is elected General Secretary.

Late November–December 2014 – Online election results for the citizen councils at the municipal level further strengthen the position of the Iglesias faction.

31 January 2015 – Beyond the Vistalegre Constituent Assembly of the autumn, a *Marcha del Cambio* (March for Change) called by Podemos draws well over 100,000 and fills the Puerta del Sol.

February–March 2015 – Alberto Rivera seems to have steered *Ciudadanos*, a nine-year-old liberal centrist party with roots in Catalonia, to upwards of 20% favorable rankings in the polls, as Podemos starts to bottom out from 28% to the low 20s. Like Podemos, Rivera's Ciudadanos (the C's) presents itself as a movement dedicated to wiping out corruption and promoting transparency. However, unlike Podemos, the C's stand for tax reductions for individuals and corporations, balanced by elimination of tax deductions and loopholes, increased flexing and loosening of labor market rules, and decreased state intervention and monopolies/oligopolies.

22 March 2015 – A snap election is provoked in the Andalucian regional parliament by Susana Díaz, PSOE Chairman of the Board of Andalucia, following a fissure in her coalition with Izquierda Unida. Both PSOE and Spanish Prime Minister Mariano Rajoy's Popular Party (PP) suffer serious drops in their polls: to 35% and 27% respectively, worst ever in Andalucia for PSOE, worst since 1990 there for PP. Podemos surges under the leadership of Teresa Rodríguez to 14.9% and 15 seats; while the C's garner 9.3% and nine seats. Together the two upstart parties get 25% of the vote, signaling the end of the era of absolute majorities in post-Franco Spanish parliamentary politics. Díaz fails to be confirmed as Chairman for two months as Podemos and Ciudadanos make demands on issues of corruption and transparency. Díaz only secures the nine C's deputies' votes for an 11 June investiture after throwing some Andalucian PSOE former leaders under the bus, raising the wrath of former PSOE Prime Minister Fernando González.

30 April 2015 – Juan Carlos Monedero, one of the founders of Podemos, resigns as one of Iglesias' leaders over differences in strategies concerning the upcoming autumn 2015 national elections. Monedero attacks the Left Keynesian drift and electoral coalition focus.

24 May 2015 – In the regional elections in 13 of 17 regions and municipal elections, Popular Unity citizen platforms *Barcelona en Comú* (Barcelona in Common) and *Ahora Madrid* (Now Madrid) surge with Podemos' support. Anti-eviction activist Ada Colau is elected mayor of Barcelona, heading a left coalition; and labor lawyer and former judge Manuela Carmena is elected mayor of Madrid in a coalition with PSOE, ending PP's long hegemony in the national capital. PSOE and PP drop from two thirds of the total vote to half. In Valencia, ecologist Joan Ribó and the left-wing politician Mónica Oltra lead a Compromise Popular Unity Platform (*Compromís*) to end two decades of PP rule, Ribó as mayor of Valencia, Oltra as vice president of the province.

13 June 2015 – The news media reports on the investiture of "Indignados mayors (who) stay true to their roots in the first day on the job." Following political party pacts, there are Popular Unity mayors in Madrid, Barcelona, Coruña, Santiago de Compostela in Galicia, Zaragoza in Aragon, and Cadiz in Andalucia. Three new Popular Unity mayors in Galicia decline the tradition of mass and religious procession accompanying investiture of mayors, tradition and practice since 1669. Pablo Iglesias seems to be trying to find his place in this Popular Unity electoral coalition surge, which he ironically started but which now seems out his control. Many claim that the Popular Unity electoral coalitions represent the most effective strategy for winning the autumn national elections. The strategy emerging is to form coalitions before, not after elections.

July 2015 – The voting intentions surveys show a triple tie between the conservatives (Partido Popular), the socialists (PSOE), and Podemos. In fourth position and far from the previous, the center-right-wing party Ciudadanos seems to play the role of a "hinge party." The current conservative government announces general elections for November or December 2015.

15–22 July 2015 – Podemos' affiliates approve the 20 December (20-D) electoral and confluence strategy. Though the implementation of this participatory process makes Podemos the first political force submitting to consultation on its strategy of alliances, this process triggers a debate on how the consultation question is posed and the participatory values in this process.

5 September 2015 – The "new mayors" for the change stress the importance of the confluence, agreement, and consensus between different political forces and social movements for a new political period and reject their "electoral use" by Podemos.

12 September 2015 – *Ahora en Común* (AeC) holds its first general assembly and defines the framework for the left-wing forces' confluence in the 20-D general elections – a Popular Unity candidature or confluence tide away from the socialist party. This platform – started by Izquierda Unida and the ecologists Equo and comprising over 1000 affiliates – also sets its ethical and programmatic premises, aiming to resemble the process followed by Ahora Madrid, Barcelona en Comú, or Zaragoza en Común for the last May local elections.

2 October 2015 – *Unidad Popular en Común* (Popular Unity in Common) emerges and attempts to build the new left-wing confluence platform placed on the left side of the PSOE, and is motivated by the argument that Ahora en Común is not being helpful to gather in Madrid the left-wing parties wanting to pact a single-list with Podemos for the 20-D general elections.

6 October 2015 – Podemos announces the "final no" of Alberto Garzón for a 20-D joint candidature and pushes him to quit

Izquierda Unida and accept integration in Podemos' list as an independent.

8 October 2015 – Barcelona en Comú and its main leader Ada Colau decide "to concur" with Confluence in the 20-D general elections. Under the label *En Comú Podem* (In Common We Can), it also includes other leftist forces such as Podem, Iniciativa per Catalunya Verds (ICV), Esquerra Unida (EUiA), and Barcelona en Comú.

10 October 2015 – In light of the breakdown in negotiations between Iglesias and Garzón, Podemos Aragón and Ahora Aragón en Común reach agreement on joint candidature for the 20-D general elections.

22–26 October 2015 – *Ahora en Común* (Now in Common) holds primary elections. Ahora en Común is created once Podemos refuse a 20-D general elections joint candidature with Izquierda Unida (IU). Alberto Garzón leads IU, replacing Cayo Lara.

Real difficulties have emerged between Ahora en Común and Podemos: (1) not all IU's members accept the union with Podemos; (2) many Podemos affiliates consider IU as part of *La Casta* or the parties from the establishment, but the left tilt of the ideological axis logic; (3) this is in contrast to Podemos' claim to be a catchall party emphasizing an "empty signifier." Consequently, IU concurs on its own with the Ahora en Común label for the 20-D general elections, but does so with barely any significant organizational or financial resources. Further, according to the regular surveys by the *Centro de Investigaciones Sociológicas* (Center of Sociological Investigations – CIS) on voting intentions, in April and July 2015 survey data there is a drift from 37.4% to 45.8% among IU's voters. IU voters respectively manifest their intention of shifting their vote to Podemos for the 20-D general elections, an enormous vote transfer in just three months.

22–26 October 2015 – Ahora en Común holds its primary elections in 25 provinces for the voting of the candidate leader to the 20-D general elections. The two main candidates are Alberto Garzón (IU's leader), the candidature called *Ahora con Alberto Garzón* (Now with Alberto Garzón), and Miguel Ángel Vázquez, *Por un Mundo Más Justo* (For a Fairer World). Among the top ten in Garzón's electoral list are popular leaders from the social, feminist, and ecologies movements, former socialists, and independent Izquierda Abierta leader Gaspar Llamazares – along with some former IU members in the Madrid environs.

27 October 2015 – Alberto Garzón's list overwhelmingly wins the Ahora en Común primaries, achieving the top five places in the candidature list for the 20-D general elections. Garzón will next vainly try to negotiate a joint bid with Podemos.

28 October 2015 – 55% of the ecologist party Equo accept a pact with Podemos for the 20-D general elections, quitting the Ahora en Común constellation.

30 October 2015 – Mayor Ada Colau of Barcelona formally announces that her party, Barcelona en Comú, by a majority of 71% will join, in Catalonia, the Confluence of Podemos, ICV (Initiative for Catalan Greens), and EUiA (United and Alternative Left, Catalunya) with the brand *En Comú Podem-En Podem Comú*, with Commissioner of Historical Memory Xavier Domenech and the founder of the anti-evictions movement (PAH) Lucia Martin at the top of the electoral list. This decision breaks with the Podemos party principle of going to the base to affirm such an alliance with another party. Podemos commits itself to Catalonia's right to decide its future in or out of Spain by referendum, and – if possible – in a new more federal plurinational Spain. Plurinational Spain is a principle of the autumn 2014 founding Podemos congress at Vistalegre.

Iglesias sacrifices central control over electoral lists and agrees to coalitions with a large degree of autonomy, reiterating the emerging upward-leaning social pacting practices. A coalition of what geographer David Harvey (2012) calls "rebel cities" is emerging out of the 15-M, PAH, and Indignados movements.

31 October 2015 – Podemos submits its 20-D elections draft political program and lists to its more than 300,000 affiliates.

2 November 2015 – Podemos wrestles with how to work with Ahora en Común – increasingly now referred to as *Unidad Popular* (Popular Unity) – while resisting its electoral lists. Podemos' dilemma is that it cannot either monopolize or organically incorporate it; and that Popular Unity appears more and more a party of what philosopher Jacques Rancière refers to as the "uncounted" – the excluded rather than the enraged (*Indignados*). Public opinion polling indicates erosion of support for Podemos due to its own questions of trust that have emerged in all its electoral wheeling and dealing. In the country as a whole, Podemos concurs respectively in a constituency-by-constituency basis with seeming rival Izquierda Unida and, with it, the Unidad Popular platform.

18 November 2015 – Colau hits the national campaign trail at rallies all over Spain to shore up support for Podemos and Popular Unity electoral list candidates.

28 November 2015 – New Mayor Joan Ribó – Valencian ecosocialist and nationalist – and his provincial vice president Mónica Oltra announce that they are joining in a Confluence with both Podemos and Popular Unity "to bring the voice of Valencia into Madrid with their own voice." Ribó argues: "There are things we cannot change from within city hall. We need a government in Madrid that helps us, rather than one that moves in the opposite direction."

16 December 2015 – The newspaper *The Guardian* reports that Colau has become the "mainstay" on the campaign trail, "pointing to the achievements of her municipal government" in efforts to arouse voters. Colau explains, "When we made it to the Government, the world did not end. The economy in Barcelona is better than ever, exports are up. We have had more tourists this summer."

19 December 2015 – Colau, Ribó, Oltra, Iglesias, Errejón, Bescama, Monedero, Enchenique, and Llamarzares all appear at a gigantic end-of-campaign rally in Valencia, draped in Podemos purple.

20 December 2015 – National Elections Results (Majority = 176 of 350):

Popular Party (PP)	29%	123 seats in Congress of Deputies
Socialist Workers (PSOE)	22%	90 seats
Podemos (P)	21%	69 seats
Ciudadanos (C's)	14%	40 seats (a drop of 6% in polls in last week)
IU/Popular Unity	4%	2 seats
Catalan Nationalists	2%	9 seats
Democracy & Freedom (DiL)	2%	8 seats
Republican Left/Catalonia Si	2%	9 seats
Basque Nationalists	1%	6 seats

23 December 2015 – Pablo Sánchez, leader of PSOE, says the election amounts to a categorical "No" to the continuation of a Mariano Rajoy-led PP government. Rajoy does not resign. Two months later Rajoy's Defense Minister refuses to answer questions in the Congress of Deputies.

28 December 2015 – PSOE, Podemos, and Ciudadanos declare opposition to Rajoy as Prime Minister.

7 January 2016 – Sánchez flies to Lisbon to visit new Portuguese Prime Minister Antonio Costa, former Lisbon mayor, who has come to power at the head of a coalition with Greens and the Left Bloc after seven inconclusive weeks following a general election at start of October 2015.

22 January 2016 – Rajoy declines the request of King Felipe VI to form a new government, as PP plus Ciudadanos only amount together to 133 seats with 176 necessary. The tradition is for the king to first ask the leader of the party with the most seats won in the last election. Sánchez and Iglesias refuse to abstain to allow a minority government, and indicate their party blocs in Congress will vote "No." Rajoy declares he will continue to be a candidate at the coming investiture as prime minister of a new government. He refuses to step down as Prime Minister or PP leader, as talk emerges of challenges to his leadership by his Vice President, Soraya Sáenz de Santamaria, and by former PP Prime Minister Manuel Aznar.

1 February 2016 – Sánchez reaches accord with Ciudadanos leader Alberto Rivera, and a Canary Islands Coalition. Iglesias refuses to endorse a PSOE-Ciudadanos government, claiming Rivera's platform is incompatible with that of Podemos and Popular Unity on issues of tax reform, labor reform, and public spending. There is debate emerging on apportioning the Bureau of the Congress of Deputies: PP 2, PSOE 2, (P) 2, C's 2. This is further complicated by arguments from the likes of parties within the Confluence umbrella like *En Marea* (Tides of) *Galicia* and *Compromís* of Valencia. Further, rumor spreads that Rivera is angling to become Speaker of the Congress – which seems to please no one. The difficult issue for Colau, Iglesias, and the Tides of Confluence is what kind of promises they can extract from Sánchez that allow the Basques, the Catalans, the Galicians, and the Valencians some part in a new "Plurinational Spain" pledged to at the Vistalegre Congress of autumn 2014. Only with Podemos serving as a federalist umbrella alliance organization do the Tides of Confluence have a political role to play on the Madrid stage, which they could never do by themselves. Errejón leads the Podemos umbrella negotiating team in talks and bargaining with Sánchez and PSOE. Spain – unlike Portugal – does not have national mass political parties, nor does Spain have confederated parties like Germany or the USA. With over 1000 regional parties in 52 provinces, this truly leads to "a soup of acronyms." (See the section titled "Spanish Political Parties" for the 40 or so significant parties in Spain.)

3 February 2016 – King Felipe VI invites Pedro Sánchez as leader of PSOE to form a government. If Sánchez can pull this off, he deserves to be Prime Minister.

12 February 2016 – In a less than cordial scene, Rajoy ignores the outstretched offer of a handshake by Sánchez.

16 February 2016 – Joan Baldovi of Compromís departs from Compromís-Podem-És el Moment to create a parliamentary group in support of Sánchez's PSOE-Ciudadanos coalition, taking four seats away from Podemos' 69 won on 20 December.

1 March 2016 – Mayor Manuela Carmena of Madrid comes out in support of a Sánchez-led government.

2 March 2016 – Sánchez appears before the Congress to present his government platform for investiture. Iglesias in his turn at the rostrum questions Sánchez's socialist values in making a deal with Ciudadanos, rather than forming a left-wing coalition. Iglesias further attacks former PSOE Prime Minister González for adopting neoliberal austerity policies in return for accession to the European Union in the 1980s, and for having the "limestone-caked" hands of a mortician for the secret assassination squads he sent out to eliminate Basque terrorists. He is followed by Domenech of En Comú who is cautioned by the Speaker that he is approaching the end of his allotted speaking time. A nonplussed Domenech in his maiden speech gently protests. On his return to his seat, Domenech is kissed on the lips by Iglesias before aghast PP deputies, in "the kiss seen round the world." Sánchez is denied – the first time a prime ministerial candidate had been denied investiture.

4 March 2016 – Allowed a second opportunity for investiture as Prime Minister, Sánchez appears two days later. Rajoy accuses him of being a "fraud." Sánchez is denied a second time. Polls indicate a second crisis of trust is brewing about Iglesias' leadership. A month before, Podemos appeared as if it would surpass PSOE if another national election was called on 26 June. Now that party slips four points and is even surpassed by Ciudadanos. Ada Colau keeps her own counsel; however, she is reported to be working on the development of her own political party at the national level.

7 March 2016 – PSOE regional leaders – in a "serious warning" to Podemos –announce that they are reconsidering all deals made with Podemos in local councils.

15–16 March 2016 – Scuffles break out within Podemos. Nine members of the Podemos Citizens' Council in Madrid engineer a vote of no confidence in regional director Luis Alegre, who is an Iglesias man. Iglesias counters the next day like a traditional

Old Left party leader by sacking Sergio Pascual, the number three person in Podemos, as Director for the Territories. Pascual is Iñigo Errejón's right-hand man. Errejón, who is leader of the Podemos/Confluence/Popular Unity negotiating team meeting with Sánchez, is known to favor entering government. He has let it be known that the Alliance must avoid "not being relegated as a left-wing fringe party to the margins of the playing board." Iglesias' show of leadership strength furthers his second crisis in trust since his strong-handed direction of the Vistalegre Congress, where he retorted to accusations: he was acting like a militant, and not – as he was accused by many – like an alpha male traditional political leader. Talk of *Pablistas* versus *Errejonistas* abounds. Errejón is said to be set to take the reins from Iglesias.

16 March 2016 – Iglesias phones Sánchez to restart negotiations in forming a government led by Sánchez. Echoing the words of Errejón and Baldovi (of Compromís), he uses the slogan "to the Valencians" to commemorate the Podemos/Popular Unity government with PSOE under Xima Puig and Mónica Oltra in Valencia the previous May. For Baldovi, the only red line is working with Rajoy and PP. For Alberto Garzón of Izquierda Unida-Ahora en Común-Popular Unity – as well as Iglesias – another red line is Rivera's Ciudadanos.

18 March 2016 – Seeking to calm troubled waters, Iglesias appoints as the new Podemos Organization Secretary Pablo Echenique – the regional director in Aragon. Echenique – an Argentinian-born Spanish physicist – is one of the Podemos MEPs elected and sent to Strasbourg in May 2014. Enchenique has great moral authority, and is linked with fellow elected MEP Teresa Rodríguez in *Sumando Podemos* (Summing Up We Can) – the more collectivist leadership faction defeated by the Iglesias/ Errejón faction *Claro Que Podemos* (Of Course We Can) which is a more democratic centralist internal party faction. Errejón does not appear with Iglesias and Enchenique; however, he is reportedly negotiating with Sánchez's team.

21 March 2016 – A biography appears: *Ada: Democratic Rebellion* by Joan Serra. Colau is quoted as saying she feels a "distance" from Iglesias whom she finds arrogant in his mode of self-expression. Further, she emphasizes that Barcelona en Comú is not Podemos. Quickly, in her own mode of damage control, Colau tells the press that she salutes Iglesias and Errejón as her best allies, and as brave companions in winning movement victories.

30 March 2016 – Iglesias reportedly removes himself as a presence in a PSOE-Podemos government headed by Sánchez, understanding that such a presence is causing great turbulence in PSOE ranks. A camera picks up Iglesias' notebook page on the table as he talks with Sánchez. His red lines are under: (1) repeal of the Rajoy labor market legal reforms and a return to those under former PSOE Prime Minister Zapatero; (2) less redistributive tax reforms than proposed earlier; (3) less public spending initiatives than proposed earlier; and (4) agreement to reduce public deficits more quickly in recognition of unease and distrust manifest in markets and the European Union. What is not in the copybook is Iglesias' continued concern for moving to a more plurinational Spain.

1–7 April 2016 – In the early days of April, Iglesias repeatedly champions the model of the "Pact of the Valencians" where Podemos in June 2015 joined in a tripartite coalition with Compromís and PSOE in Valencia to form a regional government with Xima Puig of PSOE as President and Compromís leader Mónica Oltra as Vice President. On 4 April Puig and Oltra appear in the visitors' gallery of the Congress of Deputies to focus attention on the Valentian Left Model for PSOE-Podemos negotiations. On 7 April, 24 hours after negotiations start up again, Iglesias announces, "We are not doing a deal with Ciudadanos involved...We hope PSOE will reconsider its position and enable a Government of Change." Talks break down; Iglesias promises to step aside and put the question of whether to join a coalition with PSOE and Ciudadanos to the Podemos grassroots membership in an online referendum on Thursday 14 April/Friday 15 April.

18 April 2016 – Podemos announces the results of their members' referendum. Out of 396,000 members, 149,000 vote. On the first query, 88.3% say "No" to any coalition that includes Ciudadanos. On the second query, 92% show support for a Government of the Left.

3 May 2016 – King Felipe VI receives Speaker of the Congress Patxi López, who informs him that after four months of stalled and fruitless coalition talks, there is a need to call another general election. The king dissolves the Parliament and sets 26 June (26-J) as the day for such another national election. It is the first time in the democratic epoch after Franco that the king has dissolved Parliament.

9 May 2016 – Iglesias and Alberto Garzón of Izquierda Unida announce a Joint List electoral alliance for 26-J to be called *Unidos Podemos* – uniting their two parties with 16 other leftist parties.

15 May 2016 – Fifth-anniversary celebrations in city squares of the start of the 15-M Indignados movement. Monedero and Errejón jostled by crowd in the Puerta del Sol in Madrid denouncing partisan politics.

18 May 2016 – Barcelona en Comú and Comunidad Valencia

reconstituted as Compromís announce they will be part of the Unidos Podemos electoral alliance. Ahora Madrid adds its support, respecting Mayor Carmena's decision to refrain from any campaigning.

26 May 2016 – Growing pains appear in governance for Mayor Colau in Barcelona. While recognizing the workers' right to strike, Colau takes a hard line on budgetary constraints dealing with a two-day Barcelona public metro-system strike in late February. In late May, Colau is confronted with three nights of disturbances by *Okupa* squatters who had been peacefully occupying a former bank since 2011. Colau filed for eviction, and had the bank entrance welded shut to prevent reoccupation while finding a new suitable venue for the occupiers under "social emergency housing for loss of residency" policy.

3 June 2016 – First weekend of June starts with the release in 22 Spanish theaters of Fernando León de Aranoa's film documentary on the unfolding of Podemos – *Política: Manual de Instrucciones* (Politics: Instruction Manual). The film catches the pulsating drama, the contradictions, the giddiness, the mistakes. Iñigo Errejón captures the sense of throbbing tides and flows as "having to run while our laces are untied." He also captures the empathy of audiences as an authentic leader. Polls indicate that in the 26-J campaign, Unidos Podemos has vaulted past PSOE by three to four percentage points (*el sorpasso*).

3

Mistrust/Suspicion/Betrayal and "the Provenance of Normativity"

Legitimacy in S.M. Lipset's durable definition (1981: 64) characterizes "the capacity of the (political) system to engender and maintain the belief that the existing political institutions are the most appropriate for the society." Trust, like legitimacy, is something which others attribute. It requires not just familiarity and reiterability; it requires a repetition that imbues confidence. Legitimacy provides a supporting habitus of moral justificatory resources. Accordingly, it cannot be instrumentally controlled, owned, or stored. Trust involves confidence toward the future, confidence in our expectations. The systems theorist Niklas Luhmann (1979: 10) emphasizes that "to show trust is to anticipate a future. It is to believe as though the future was certain." Trust functions to sustain expectation of expectations, to reduce uncertainty and risk.

For Jürgen Habermas (1975), legitimacy involves a sense of the worthiness to be recognized as authority, a worthiness demonstrated in a process of interrogating, testing, and critically evaluating normative appeals. It involves a perception of that which must not be open to a sense of suspicion or, worse, a sense of betrayal. Legitimacy involves a resonant sense of connection, a resonant perception of an expanded shared empathy. This is a resonant sense of mutual self-bindingness, and of acting together intersubjectively as a putative "We" with an institutionalizing orientation (Iacoboni, 2008). Mistrust gives the justification for breaking off or changing familiar paths, and shaping new ones, what Luhmann refers to as dismissing the familiar while creatively anticipating a horizon.

For Habermas (1975: 60), "legitimation crisis" refers to

destabilizing impasses and trauma within the interdependency of the sociocultural system, the political-administrative system, and the economic system. Mistrust of a regime loosens any sense of integrative capacity of its normative structure, and consequently its processes of conflict regulation and consensus formation. A later Habermas (1996) saw the capability to resolve crisis tendencies as a consequence of the systemic "colonization" of the public sphere, a phenomenon he related to the democratic/ legitimation deficit inherent in the European Union.

Unlike Luhmann, for Habermas trust in normativity is not just reiterable cognitive expectation of expectations. It is both a cognitive and affective confidence in a constituted normativity as a practical accomplishment, that is, the meaning-making involved in the forms of life and practices we create intersubjectively. As Hans Lindahl (2007, 2014) adds, the "constitutive provenance" of normative orders is not just a secondary derivative feature, but a constitutive process where we act together to articulate an emergent institutionalizing imaginary. A circle of repetition is broken, producing something singular and new, some novel emergent forms and practices.

In terms of the Indignados movement, these novel emergent forms may not be familiar in the context of the post-Franco Transition State, but familiar in Spanish traditions of syndicalist practices going back to the 1920s/30s and to the nineteenth century. These are anti-authoritatian/anti-hierarchical sentiments – outside either Leninist or Social Democratic paths – rooted in mutual aid association, workers' self-management, and both regionalism and federalism. Its institutional embodiment to this day is the Confederación Nacional de Trabajo (CNT), in contrast with the communist-aligned Confederación Sindical de Comisiones Obreras (CCOO.), or the Unión General de Trabajodores (UGT) aligned with the Socialists (Partido Socialista Obrero Español –PSOE).

Spain – a state more than a nation – is afflicted with multiple legitimation crises. First, there is the 2008 crisis of autonomous global finance, a crisis in the financialization of everyday life where capacity is mortgaged to salvage future needs, where consumers are manipulated to become addicted to credit (Kjaer, Teubner, and Febbrajo, eds, 2011). Second, there is the persistent legitimation crisis Habermas wrote about in 1975: the crisis of the Keynesian welfare state – rather than the financial Keynesianism of the neoliberal epoch. In Spain, a later developing paternalistic Franco welfare state with promises of *embourgeoisement* has been put at risk, where risk itself – rather than solidarity – becomes the dominant motivating force. Third, there is the legitimation crisis of the post-Franco constitutional state, and the re-emergent memory of the promise of attempts at republicanism. Sebastian Royo (2014) notes other legitimation crises: the stagnant wages of the middle class; the growing social inequality; the inability to sustain welfare benefits; the decline of the trade unions; and the failure of the education system to adapt to new technology and market need.

The crises became clearly manifest in 2007/8 with the collapse of the savings and loan credit unions (*cajas, caixas*) linked with real estate bubbles and renewable energy bubbles. This ultimately led to a European Union 100 billion euro bail-out and European Central Bank-monitored rescue plan. The *cajas* started in the nineteenth century as pawn shops, not for generating profit for shareholders like commercial banks. Of 45 that existed at the start of 2007, only two remain. The rest have been either taken over by the government or forced into bank mergers that resulted in wiping out the equity holders at the start of 2007. There emerged a sense of perceived collusion between elites at the command posts of the political-administrative and economic systems to concoct schemes to "extract resources" from taxpayers for their own benefit while colonizing the *cajas* to provide easy credit to prop up consumer demand.

Deeper, as Sofia Pérez (1997) notes, there persists an

oligopolistic structure of a private banking cartel with the enduring Spanish imperial state, whose bureaucracy maintained interventionist control over the economy. The *Franquismo* State copied Mussolini's statist corporatism with its chambers and goal of economic autarky, a goal only abandoned in 1959 so as to become integrated into international markets and to facilitate foreign investment. After 1986 with entry into the European Economic Community, foreign banks were allowed to enter the Spanish credit industry. Prime Minister Felipe González (of PSOE) shifted bank resources in the1980s into public debt financing.

While bringing on a universalizing public health care system and extending the public education system, González is linked to banking elites like Miguel Boyer and Carlos Solchaga who are more determined to reduce inflation than unemployment. In the agreement to enter the European Union, González accepts the condition of flexing up labor law reforms, deregulating the labor market, as well as dismantling the country's industrial infrastructure – thus eroding its working-class organization. This results in a rise of temporary contract and vendor work, and a decline in the influence of trade unions. At the same time, housing rentals are deregulated.

There was no radical break with Franquismo state corporatism in the Moncloa Pact of 1978, orchestrated by Prime Minister Adolfo Suárez and detailing the Transition from Franco authoritarian rule. To what extent was the Moncloa Pacted Transition a mere adaptation of the persistent cartelization, using televisual logic? This is the argument made by Juan Carlos Monedero (2011) in his book *The Transition Told to Our Parents: The Night of Spanish Democracy*. To what extent was the Pacted Transition what Juan Linz and Alfred Stepan (1996, Chapter 6) describe as a regime-initiated transition of "limited pluralism"? This is a pluralism of mutual institutional guarantees among "segments of society" rather than a negotiated democracy: seeking to reflect social balances (including Falangists like Manuel Fraga), limiting political competition and access to the policy arena so as to control the agenda.

"Everything was on a clean slate": crimes of the Franco Era were forgiven and reconciliation was the theme so as to enable the newly approved 1978 Constitution to be launched. Monedero refers to this as "collective amnesia recycled as 'tolerant democracy'," an amnesia where the experiences of the Second Republic of the 1930s is left to oblivion. The PSOE along with Santiago Carrillo's Partido Comunista Español (PCE) were asked to keep mobilization in the streets to a minimum so that the pacts would have a chance of success. These two parties assisted with the unions in containing conflict in workplaces. By 1989, PSOE was moving into positions that were more and more pro-business and constraining of labor – a seeming reconstituted civil society with emergent democratic values. But as César Molinas argues in *What to Do with Spain: The Theory of Spain's Political Class* (2013), a reconfigured/rejigged political caste (*La Casta*) came to "colonize" the Constitutional Courts, the Bank of Spain, and the General Council of the Judiciary.

A sense of mistrust, suspicion, and betrayal in Spain especially is triggered by the perception that the leaders of the two political parties PP and PSOE are *poseurs*. They pose insincerely as "socially concerned" in their promotional communication and marketing, while actually operating the other way. It is a manipulating of discourse and legitimation claims in a misleading way. We can refer to it as *social washing* akin to whitewashing and greenwashing.

In the Spanish case – as well as in those of Portugal and Italy – traditional conservative and social democratic parties seek to secure their base in the middle classes and low-income social groups. Social washing characterizes their official discourse as they try to stay in power or attain power, while implementing unpopular antisocial austerity.

As Wolfgang Streeck (2014: 61) notes, the term "legitimation crisis" was originally used by Habermas (1975) and Offe (1984) in the 1970s to describe how the capitalist state could no longer meet the demands for more democracy, for more society. Still, the concept of legitimation crisis has now had a shelf-life of four decades in a broad sense. Capital endeavored to win back the confidence of markets.

Legitimation crisis and legitimation deficit have come to characterize:

- discontent about perceived unfairness of institutions of governance which are seen as perpetuating a regime of favors and influence;
- disaffection with perceived institutional degeneration marked by inefficient performance, non-responsiveness, inconsistency, and corruption; and
- discrediting of a privileged/exclusive political class's "right to rule."

In Spain, the crises of legitimacy are deeper than the effects of the 2008 economic crisis. Deeper is a sense of unfulfilled democratic promises and a declining trust in the institutions of the Transition State set up in 1977/8. In 1989, a new daily newspaper appeared, *El Mundo*, with the declared purpose of uncovering and investigating in detail every scandal in the institutions of governance (Humblaeck, 2015: 139). Beyond the privilege, the cronyism, and the corruption, the tides of social insertion argue for the need for reconstituting the social basis of legitimacy. New trust networks were committed to re-embedding the social, and overflowing the familiarism that hindered the development of paradigmatic reforms toward universalism in the domains of health care, education, and the welfare state (Calzada and del Pino in Guillén and León, 2011:

139–64; Guillén, 2010; Esping-Andersen, 1990, 1999). The overflowing is indeed – as Walter Benjamin teaches us – a swelling beyond the limits of its epoch, and a displacement superimposing a new threshold (Eiland, 2001, 2014).

To a great extent, in the early years of the Transition State, the political class (*La Casta*) had been willing to work together and overcome differences in the pursuit of public goods and the need to innovate. The public was willing to tolerate the institutions of governance becoming colonized by *La Casta* in a Spanish patron-client sense of state-ness – but only so long as they benefited from this. Any semblance of democracy was said to have "frozen" and to be in need of "defrosting" (Threlfall, 2008; Guillén, 2010).

Following Niklas Luhmann (1984, 1990a, 1990b, 1992) the state form is an ensemble of practices which interrelates and reconciles contingently with a sense of self-referentiality for the purpose of coordinating the mobilization and allocation of resources. Like any state form, the Transition State's legitimacy as a regime is a contingent formation, to be called upon to generate within itself justifications for the purported *common binding decisions* it must make. These are made with its plausible normative sense of self-reference *vis-à-vis* its environments of social and cultural systems as well as the circuitry of power grounded in exchange value and capital accumulation.

Following Antonio Gramsci (2011) and J.P. Nettl (1968), we can understand the state form in the integral sense of the whole system of political operations, the whole corporate machinery of rule interrelating the associations of civil society with a "historical bloc" controlling the institutional command posts of political society. The normative self-reference point of the Transition State, as an integral institutional ensemble of rule-making, is not some basic norm. Nor is it some self-referential decisionism of a leader. Rather, it is the shared values which precede the acceptance of political decisions.

For John Dewey in *The Public and Its Problems* (1927), the state form must always be rediscovered in terms of some rationale: of how it can be used to provide a framework to facilitate social learning; of how it can be capable of reshaping the whole of society so as to facilitate it according to the antecedent patterns and norms of a trust regime.

In his 1990 book *Democracy's Voices*, Robert Fishman points out a paradox: that in Spain there is a higher incidence of collective protests than elsewhere in Europe. Yet when it comes to the ballot box, these protests prove to end up "disengaging" rather than "engaging" the public sphere, eliciting more disappointment despite their large list of grievances. The narrative of the Indignados, from PAH through Podemos and Popular Unity Confluence, attempts to recover, reclaim, and redeem "the social" and change such a disappointing electoral path dependency.

4

Confluence toward Contesting the Transition State

"No somos mercancias en manos de politicos ni banqueros."
(We are not mere things to be manipulated by politicians and bankers.)

The above quotation is another popular slogan from the 15-M Indignados movement's condemnation of the illegitimacy, cronyism, and corruption in the Transition State and the search for a new politics.

Our timeline reveals:

- presence;
- a genealogy of decentered critical practices mediated by new autonomous social forms and bonds; and
- a later coordination for urban, regional, and national electoral purposes.

Pushing us beyond just a focus on the economic crisis of 2008 to one of deep regime legitimacy deficits, the Indignados movement raises the salient issue: Whether these latter regime deficits are fixable in the Transition State?

Transition is the process by which an old regime abandons the most notable characteristics of its institutional arrangement to a new regime.

The first post-Franco *transition state form* amounts to only a surface dismantling by the political establishment of the de-legitimated Franco Vertical Syndicate. There was not a rupture with that past, but a reformist opening to the trade union movement and the Left with a project of social partnerships and concertation on the Western European neocorporatist model. No longer under the obsession with the ideological trauma of the Civil War, might a Confluence contesting the Transition State's legitimation deficits lead to a *second transition state form*? This could be a state form that would be in coordinative alignment with socio-economic assemblies and mutualities (*mutualités* of social soclidarity) responsive to the new complexities of economic development...and perhaps the plurinational realities of the peoples of Spain?

"Contestation" is the generic term in the genealogical approach to valuation/legitimation claims. It involves opening up the faults, fissures, fractures, and ruptures, and at the same time opening up the alternative legitimation claims – opening up the possibilities. In our grasping of the interiority of movement committedness as a mode of legitimation, we present an unfolding genealogy of practice-based forms and frameworks of knowledge creating new critical spaces by the autonomous tides of social insertion/reinsertion.

In the sociology of Alain Touraine (1977, 1981, 1988, 2009) we understand social movements in terms of institutionalizing leverage:

- seizing control of the field of historicity into which we are thrown;
- creating new frames and spaces of social possibility and new bonds of solidarity; and
- seeking to recognize state forms of wielding power and establishing codes and protocols.

Ultimately, social movements' classic dilemma is whether to enter into political institutions and assume institutional responsibilities or to keep acting as a pressure group.

Confluence involves weaving together a decentered/ decentralized meshwork (Delanda, 1997, 1998) of connected-up practices as new social spaces – here critical citizens' practices in the form of digital platforms, grassroots initiatives, occupations, assemblies/circles – rather than some unitarian/ monistic ideological partisan aggregation. This Confluence among the autonomous movements within the umbrella concept of Indignados signifies a counternarrative of the Social Subjects of Rights to that of the neoliberal sense of dissociated private subjectivity (cf. Chari, 2016).

Confluence is a coming together:

- to build trust networks for health debating and deliberating;
- to subvert the normal distribution of spaces;
- to open up critical space to empower the Social Subjects of Rights wherein subjects find themselves; and
- to provide leverage capabilities to transcend crossings of the several layers and scales of order, duty, and obedience, including the "scaling up" of the sharing of local initiatives based on reciprocity.

In Gramscian terms, the movements' collaborative practices dissolve entrenched nested hierarchies and re-mediate the social field with new democratic forms and new horizontally networked spaces of trust. These are spheres of engagement consolidating a new form of democracy that re-embeds/reinserts the social in the sense of sharing responsibility in adapting to and managing risk in an epoch of increasing vulnerability.

The concept of "social insertion" has roots in the *muncipalismo* of mutual aid practiced by Spanish anarchists and anarchosyndicalists since the middle of the nineteenth century, although it is used in new ways by the Indignados. The contemporary movement argues for and establishes a solidarity-based economy in a way not set down by state institutions. Here we have Podemos leaders and Ada Colau's Barcelona en Comú examine closely the state's institutionalizing power – despite a residual distrust of the state. They seek to leverage the state in the tradition of *municipalismo* – as well as in its distrust of backroom dealing in Popular Front coalitions, and fear of the embourgeoisement of the peasantry and the proletariat (Bookchin, 1977; Dolgoff, 1971).

The rebellion of General Franco's military to start the Civil War was bent on the extirpation of *municipalismo*. Franco's appeal was to the "folk soul" of the Spanish. Franco's mission was to smash the trade union movements as well as the re-emergence in 1930s Spain of cooperatives and mutual aid cooperatives, rallying the peasantry by seizing land and then giving it away to the peasantry. The landowners' mortgages were held by powerful banks supporting Franco.

The new forms of local and horizontal collaborative initiatives of social reinsertion/re-embeddedness are often referred to today by economists as *sustainable community movement organizations* (SCMOs). They are characterized by their exploring alternative forms of and spaces for solidarity-based exchange and consumption – by rebuilding new social relationships with intent on some radical revision of the market; by disrupting the assimilated neoliberal understandings of how we consume goods and services. Examples include new consumer/producer cooperatives, barter groups, local currencies, ethical banking, time banks, and urban gardening (Pais et al., 2016; Gold, 2004). The digital platforms attached to such initiatives spread a network understanding of the ways and means of the recirculating of goods, the sharing of productive assets, and exchanging itself.

This is a counter-movement contrary to Margaret Thatcher's rant that "there is no alternative" (TINA) to the neoliberal project of structural readjustment beyond the "wetness" of the social democratic "nanny state." In a sense, it is the *double movement* described by Karl Polanyi (1944, 1971; cf. Dale, 2010) by which society knows how to defend and protect itself and its basic needs with its own reappropriating alternatives to an excessively commodified environment (cf. Beckert, 2007; Block and Somers, 1984). The SCMOs, reinserting/re-embedding bonds and norms of reciprocal solidarity, horizontally orchestrate islands of embodied engagement. They harken to a new transition, what we will come to refer to as a "socially pacted transition," as opposed to the political pacts of elites that characterize the First Transition of the Moncloa Agreements and the experiments in concertation. This is a reciprocal solidarity of shared responsibility rather than the Durkheimian functional solidarity that characterizes the administrative socially protective welfare state.

A new form of social partnership and *social pacting* characteristic of the SCMOs emerges since the 1990s (Ebbinghaus, 2006), beyond the older mutual aid of *municipalismo* – as a new stage of associational mutual self-limiting connecting protocolism. Or as we might say: "How we come to code our mutual self-reference." Not what Lehmbruch (1998) labeled a *negotiated democracy* as a corporatist social partnership. These are bootstrapping practices of benchmarking, as well as common resource and information pooling – triggered rolling rule-updating, and institutionalized signal thresholds for inspections and sanctions (Willke, 2007; Sabel, 1994). They involve what Sabel has referred to as "social learning by mutually monitoring."

These recursive new social pacts are referred to by Karin Bäckstrand (2006) as *multi-stakeholder social pacts* (MSSPs). Affected stakeholders come together as *reciproqueteurs* – in the sense of Elinor Ostorm's *common goods* social economics – rather than as privatized/dissociated entrepreneurs. They establish endogenous self-reflective deliberative processes. Further, they encourage mutual learning by the reciproqueteurs working in these new forms of social partnership from the bottom up. This is not some "sharewashing" shifting risk to employees under the guise of "sharing." The new form of social pact constituting the SCMO is understood as a decentered interlaced hybrid network of self-regulation and mutual monitoring. International Monetary Fund (IMF) structural adjustment programs dealing with public debt have ironically forced many communities to develop and strengthen creative autonomous local SCMOs. Karl Polanyi's double movement indeed.

Describing the context of the Transition State

Contesting the state here involves opening critical spaces in responding to the unfolding/enfolding of the twenty-first-century political economy. The Transition State itself is the beginning of the "normalization" of the Spanish State in the Western democracies of the emergent European Union of the 1980s. Significantly, the eminent historian of Spanish fascism Stanley Payne (1993) titled his book on the Second Spanish Republic of 1931–6: *Spain's First Democracy*.

For centuries, Spain scarcely developed a democratic culture. There was a short-lived First Republic in 1873, and then a messy stillborn and unconsolidated Second Republic that was beleaguered by numerous regional conflicts, anticlerical sectarianism, a mosaic of fragmented political parties with little capability of compromising, and elements of the labor movement that opposed the Republic.

Already in 1932, rebellious plotters against the Second Republic had been having meetings with Italo Balbo, Mussolini's Minister of the Air Force and a former Black Shirt leader. These and other anti-Republican plotters arranged to provide General Franco in Spanish Morocco with a fleet of transport planes to link up with anti-Republican strongholds on the Iberian mainland. Not to go unnoticed were the sizable number of priests in Catalonia and the Basque Country who aligned with the Republic in its promise to respect autonomous governments among the diverse Spanish peoples.

In place of the Republic, the victorious Franco established what was termed an "organic democracy" wherein workers were incorporated in the non-voluntarist Vertical Syndicate (*Sindicato Vertical*) that prescribed compulsory representation of both workers' and employers' associations. Trade union confederations like the anarchosyndicalist CNT (*Confederación Nacional del Trabajo*) and the socialist UGT (*Unión General de Trabajadores*) went underground. Such a framework would be opened up in the Caudillo's last decade, 1965–75. A statist organized corporatism was grounded in the privileged places in the New Order for the Catholic Church and the military with the purpose of constraining and suppressing class conflict. In Franco's obsession with order, centralized provincial intendents (*caciques*) were turned to, reflecting the centuries-old tradition of the centralized Castilian State's administrative prefects/ prefectures rather than the self-governance of civil society associations. Indeed, in the 1940s and 1950s, it would be strictly forbidden to organize any form of independent voluntary associations. This was a cartelized state apparatus pockmarked by cronied family networks.

In the midst of World War II, Franco structured Spain as a political economy of autarky, from which it was ultimately pushed out in 1959 by the United States, the International Monetary Fund, and Opus Dei, with apolitical technocrats replacing the fascist political class installed in 1939. Franco's Vertical Syndicate was now out of step with economic and social realities. A Stabilization Plan was initiated with Franco's approval. It sparked a significant amount of development and created the basis for Spain's transition to a modern market society. The Stabilization Plan also brought on a new breed of political class – many of them members of Opus Dei – who were policy wonks bent on turning out economic development plans.

A Spanish economic miracle (*el milagro español*) ensued, lasting until 1974 with an associated Second Embourgoisement – not of the civilizing process of manners, fashion, and politeness described by Norbert Elias (1939). This First Embourgeoisement emerged in Spain during the middle of the nineteenth century, as chronicled by Jesus Cruz (2011). A Second Embourgeoisement comes to pass between 1959 and 1974; this time it is the restyling of the working and white-collar classes in what was becoming at the same time one of Europe's weakest welfare states. Spain's economic growth rate during that period was second only to Japan's, and by the middle 1970s it became the ninth largest economy in the world, just behind Canada. Obviously a sudden economic spurt, yet it was inadequately secured by a welfare state. The boom was halted by the petroleum and stagflation crises of the 1970s.

By 1971, the political class (*La Casta*) of the Franco regime recognized that there was a need for some semblance of a political party system. By 1977, following Franco's death, independent trade unions and business associations would be legalized along with the political parties. Within a year, also legalized was CC.OO. (Confederación Sindical de Comisiones Obreras), organized in the 1960s in a clandestine manner by the Communist Party (PSE) as well as by Catholic Worker. CC.OO. had been leading illegal strikes against the Franco regime. In 1971, under Proceso 1001, CC.OO. leaders were jailed as subversives for over a year. CC.OO. persisted in tactics of penetration: infiltration and insertion – boring from within – into the Vertical Syndicate, culminating in union elections in 1975, and in involvement with the PCE in the Moncloa Constitutional Pacts of 1977, creating Transition State apparata with the intent of leading Spain to democracy.

With the prolonged prosperity, and a Second Embourgeoisement, came not only the promise of democratization, but also a rejection of labor radicalism, and an increasing emphasis on social mobility and focus on "lifestyle": democratization as the consumer society. All this erupts and mushrooms in the years following Franco's death, as depicted in the cinema of Pedro Almodóvar.

After Franco, the political class morphed a bit more under the leadership of Adolfo Suárez, who was more liberal than the old Franquists in the military, calling for the legalization of the Communist and Socialist Workers political parties and Spain's first free elections since 1936. Suárez had climbed to the top of *La Casta*, rising to be Deputy General Secretary of Franco's pseudo-political party, the National Movement (*Movimiento Nacional*) with strong links to Opus Dei. The Movimiento, like the Vertical Syndicate, was dismantled. Rather than resist the democratic transition, former Franquist leaders reinvented themselves as new centrists. Elected to a four-year term in 1977, Suárez put together a party with liberals and social democrats called UCD (Unión de Centro Democrático) but faced increasing competition from Felipe González's revised Socialist Workers Party (PSOE).

The Moncloa Constitutional Accords of 1977 focused not just on economic stabilization so as to enable the adaptation of a concertation – like West Germany's political economy. It also created a climate favorable to constituting democratic institutions. A most powerful Falangist minister under Franco, Manuel Fraga endeavored mightily for an authoritarian Ordoliberalism, reminiscent of the theorizing of Carl Schmitt (cf. Cristi, 1998). The focus was on shaping a societal consensus to support the legitimacy of the Transition State. The leader of the newly legitimated Communists (PCE), Santiago Carrillo, sought to avoid the intervention of the military, the security forces, and the courts – none of which had yet been reformed. Such a climate contributed to the moderation of demands on all sides – even among regional nationalists advocating greater autonomy or even independence. There was an agreement to look forward rather than to look back to the trauma and persistent animosities of the Civil War – even to amnesty both the hardened and incendiary supporters and foes of the Franco regime (Field, 2009: 379-80, 395; cf. Field, 2005).

For Ramón Cotarelo (1996, 2011, 2015) and Juan Carlos

Monedero (2011) the Transition State was a restoration of the Bourbon state form without Franco. This was not a *pacta ruptura*, breaking with the past, nor was it a democratic social pacting. It was a political pact involving party elites consulting with their key constitutents in emergent civil society associations (Encarnación, 2001). The political pact-making practices of the previous authoritarian regime persisted – facilitating elite rule and depressing access to positions of leadership. Significantly, despite his opening to the liberals and social democrats, Suárez sought to eliminate Marxists from the economic ministries (Encarnación, 1997: 409).

A seeming consolidation of democracy had been achieved with the victories of Felipe González and the PSOE in October 1982, followed by wins in 1986, 1989, and 1993 – and accession into the European Economic Community (EEC), predecessor to the European Union (EU). However, González mines the cult of personality (*personalismo*), a staple of Spanish political culture. *Felipismo* seemingly too easily becomes entangled in yet a new form of corrupt cronyism involving "supportive" family networks.

By 1987/8, the concertation project is breaking down as it is viewed by the so-called social partners as too expensive. González's PSOE divorces itself from the UGT's call for a general strike. This break and legitimation deficit is not soley due to the Transition itself, but possibly due to the influence of the then West German Social Democratic Party (SPD) as well, which had nurtured the resurgent PSOE. Nancy Bermeo (1994) described how González's embrace of neoliberalism was something that Suárez's UCD had not dared to carry out in terms of labor market reforms. The trade unions were understandably unwilling to sign national accords without promises to mitigate the high social cost of economic liberalization.

Was there an intent on a sequential strategy: democratization followed by concertation as an adapted form of the Spanish pacting tradition? Or was the mutual reference point in the Transition State's democratizing satisfying the EEC accession requirements? Was economic liberalization overarching all along?

While the winds of global finance propelled the disproportionate bubble economy of the first decade of our twenty-first century, Spain continued to be marked by low salaries, a regressive tax/fiscal system, and a perverse growth model fueled by the exploitation of cheap labor and increasingly precarious employees in activities that in many instances take place in the informal economy. So when the housing bubble burst, the Socialist government of Prime Minister José Luis Rodríguez Zapatero fell into elite settlements with the diktats of the IMF and EU without consulting civil society leaders and the public in any collaborative deliberation and negotiation. The Zapatero regime of the Transition State was perceived to be responding to the demands and interests of supranational and transnational elite actors – cleaning up a corrupted system of public finance and incurred foreign debts at the cost of social spending and depressing wage conditions. What Zapatero started is continued by his conservative rival and successor from the Popular Party, Mariano Rajoy.

A newer generation in Spain seems less bound both by political pacting by elites and by a pervasive fear of political instability that marked the generation of the First Transition. To that extent, a good degree of democratization has already been consolidated, even though residues of the familiarism, privilege, and cronyism characterizing patron-client politics rather than concertation persist.

In 1994, Popular Party leader and soon-to-be Prime Minister José Maria Aznar (1996–2004) wrote a book called *España: La Segunda Transición*, arguing that the PSOE was not the natural party of government in the Transition State, that contrary to a tolerant federalism there should be a consolidation of the autonomies in a strong federal state, and that Spain needs to be following more Mrs Thatcher's drive to make the labor market more flexible and to commodify social services. By the end of the first decade of the new century, the term "the Second Transition" was being used to characterize his PSOE successor Zapatero's dedication to gender equality, gay rights, multiculturalism, and expanding regional autonomy (Mathieson, 2007; Field, 2010). But Zapatero could scarcely deal with problems of unemployment, precarity, and exploited cheap labor. Cotarelo (2005) argues that Prime Minister Rajoy after 2011 engages in regressive Franquist politics that defeats the spirit of the Transition. Perhaps the Confluence – as a horizontally socially pacted transition aligned with electoral politics sparked by the Indignados – can lead to change in the state form of that first Transition itself.

5

"No Future for You": Recalling André Gorz

In the context of the economic crisis taking place since 2007 in Europe and abroad, the purported aim of the so-called "austerity policies" was to reactivate the economy and employment mostly in southern European countries. The reduction of labor market rigidities and the severe narrowing of the welfare state's dimensions track back to the austerity diktats of the IMF and the EU, together with the particularities implemented by each national government.

The 1978 Constitution emanating from the Moncloa Pacts in Article 1 defines Spain as "a social and democratic State, subject to the rule of law." The Spanish Social Model of the universal provision of social rights has been becoming restricted to those contributing to social security accounts and has become, as a result of austerity policies, under "permanent strain" (Pavolini, León, Guillén, Ascoli, 2014; Guillén, 2013).

Spain has always stood way back in terms of equality and the welfare state. Spain's first social security act only came in 1963. As Esping Andersen (1999: 81) noted, Spanish social services are "familiarist," that is, oriented toward the support of traditional family roles. The social services are reliant on taxes for financing, and social policies that grew dramatically from the late 1970s were often regressive. The Spanish Social Model has a Bismarckian type of social security system, a social democratic universalism when it comes to health and education, and residual liberalism in minimum income measures (see Palier, 2008). That model has been changing its interpretation of social rights to a more restricted one, for example with regard to health care assessed in terms of individual contribution to social security accounts.

The Indignados articulate claims as a response to declining expectations in employment and life chances. The labor and social policy reforms initiated by the government of Spain and the European Union signify an end to the goals of *embourgeoisement* associated with the 1959–74 economic boom and the establishment of a Spanish welfare state with relatively "patchy safety nets" (Guillén and León, 2011) within the democratic consolidation under the PSOE governments of Felipe González – but a welfare state marked by a clear neoliberal social model.

What the González Government could not tackle was the structural problem of unemployment/underemployment as well as what Olivier Blanchard and Lawrence Summers (1986) referred to as the hysteresis effects of being out of work so long that expectations and lifestyle diminish. The ability of the Spanish national government to increase redistribution of wealth through the fiscal system stopped in the middle 1990s, when means-testing became increasingly used. Means-tested programs result in difficulties for the lower middle class, whose income is too high to access public programs, but also too low to buy services in the market.

Labor precarity becomes a stable pattern, especially after the Rajoy Government's 2012 labor market law reforms enhancing the capacity of employers to unilaterally modify employees' working conditions. Labor becomes less stable. Workers are less protected. Salaries are pushed down. Temp jobs proliferate: going from one temporary job to another – with interns competing with contract labor. Precarity extends to access to housing, evictions, and permanent indebtedness. Access to education – always with a large amount of private tuition – has become more restricted than ever.

For a younger generation socialized to expect the bringing of ever-improving conditions, expectations now seem unfulfillable. Uncertainty hangs over them like a shroud. Already in 2006, there emerged an Assembly against Precarity and for Dignified

Housing (*Asemblea contra la Precariedad y por la Vivienda Digna*).

At present, in the case of Spain, evidence proves the unjust character of the approach to the economic crisis – one that widens the socio-economic differences and the ideological basis of these policies. Thus, the level of unemployment is 25% in general – 52% among the young between 18 and 35, over 60% for those between 18 and 24; also, according to Intermon Oxfam's report "An Economy for the 1%" (2015), Spain is the OECD country with the fastest-growing inequality since the beginning of the crisis, just behind Cyprus, while 14 times the cascading rate of finequality in Greece.[1]

Spain already had the lowest social expenditures per capita in the inner 15 of the EU. Thus, it is already somewhat difficult to talk of a dismantling of the welfare state and consequently policies for social protection and well-being of millions of citizens (issues such as health, education, housing, work).

Whereas Paris in 1968 witnessed a challenge to the technocratic social democratizing state, post-2007 Madrid involves a growing *Precariat* and some of the highest unemployment rates, as the state deflects social problems back on society. Under the severe economic crisis of 2008 caused by the bursting of the 1992–2007 bubble economy[2] and the subsequent austerity policy of welfare state cuts, a generation born after 1985 has no expectations of social mobility, access to their parents' values of *embourgeoisement*, or furthermore to a secured predictable near future. This generation finds itself cut off from circuits of capital accumulation, from institutions of collective bargaining, from workplaces as pillars of twentieth-century social democracy, and from working-class parties allied to welfare state policies.

In this chapter we resurrect the implications of André Gorz's theorizing in the wake of the eclipse of the once bright future of Spain's fledgling democracy, addressing the next three subjects:

(1) There is outrage among the youth raised under the welfare

state public policies, but also among their parents and grandparents who experienced the transition from Franco's dictatorship regime to democracy. They currently see how relative life security suddenly turns into confusion and uncertainty, worried not just for themselves but, even before that, for their relatives. In this context, citizens wonder to what extent they have been accomplices in the bubble and its bursting, considering either their consumption patterns (and in general their lifestyles) or their electoral preferences. Their seemingly comfortable positions derived from delegating the nation's fate to the political class, without having to wonder about how the underlying processes of the economy were actually working.

(2) The data gathered by the Centro de Investigaciones Sociológicas (CIS) over the last 16 years on Spanish public opinion leaves no doubt about the constant decline of citizens' trust in core institutions for democratic life such as politics, the government, and the economy. We assert that the evidence of this social delegitimization process of the democratic system has high explanatory strength for the understanding of the Indignados outrage that broke out in the year 2011.

(3) The "Outraged" symbolize the search for alternative ways of social interaction, intersubjectivity, and networks guided by horizontal and rhizomatic principles that make possible a higher control of living conditions by individuals and communities, and in opposition to the tendency in contemporary societies toward "total institutions" – where the government appears to be responsible: (a) for a seeming lack of initiative and control to prevent or manage the crisis; and (b) for their dependency on austerity measures coming from "outside."

Recalling André Gorz

We turn to revisit Gorz's central notion of non-class – *Farewell to the Working Class* (1980/82) – for the interpretation of the emergence of a new generation of grandchildren significantly affected by the stunting of the welfare state and the externally imposed austerity policies in Spain.

Gorz's post-1980s ecological Marxist writings leave us other relevant ideas we consider, particularly his promoting of networks of cooperatives and of repair workshops which would benefit from the emergence of "peer production" that anticipates the commons movement associated with Elinor Ostrom.

Reflecting on his long association with the journal *Les Temps Moderns* with its commitment to the proletariat as the revolutionary subject of historicity, and outraged by the French Communist Party's betrayal of the 1968 movement for social self-management, Gorz posed the dissolution of the working class itself as the bearer of the remaking of history. It had become a working class without a sense of transcendent collective identity, without any interest in creating a society based on the autonomous production of use-values rather than exchange-values. Labor was understood as "work": something one has, rather than what one does. Labor had become integrated in the cycle of production and consumption of commodities.

Sociologically, Philip Selznick in *TVA and the Grass Roots* had posed this seeming recurrence of Robert Michels' "iron law of oligarchy" in the labor movement as the way in which labor movement unions and parties attain relative autonomy from those who give them their mandate. But Gorz gives up the ghost, and returns to a more ecologically based anarchosyndicalist conception very much evident in the "direct action" strategy of David Graeber (2002, 2009) in Occupy Wall Street, and in the Commons Movement described by Ugo Mattei and Saki Bailey (2013).

Gorz broke with the "all or nothing" approach of the

Proletarian Left, in its negotiated involvement in the capitalist process, and its accommodation with productivism. He pierced the veils of technological progress of post-industrial society theorists like Alain Touraine and Daniel Bell to discern: (1) the steady rising unemployment; (2) the emergence of a large strata of precarious employment of temps, part-timers, or flex-time workers, and with it the disintegration of full-time wage labor; (3) the desperate attempts at resurrecting corporatist corpses; and (4) the degradation and disintegration of the culture of the workplace.

On the other hand, Gorz asserted (1983, 2010, 2012) that the new microtechnology of the post-industrial epoch: (1) does not automatically lend itself to the regeneration of capitalist accumulation; (2) does not give capitalists incentive to continue the conflict-regulation approach to workplace life; and (3) no longer links exchange-value relations to labor time and the right to having a job (cf. Sklar, 1988).

Ironically, Gorz argued that new opportunities emerge for socialism in a capitalism strong enough to reproduce itself, but not strong enough "to fulfill and generalize promises of bourgeois human development" (see Gindin, 2004.) These are opportunities related to cooperatives – what has come to be called "commons activities" – as the prefigurative basis, not of a homogeneous Proletarian Subject of Rights, but of heterogenous Social Subjects of Rights that corresponded to the needs of reciprocity and complexity in the emergent transnational society of networks crossing the nation-state borders of a *depassé* Westphalian system.

In *Farewell* (p. 72), Gorz was able to anticipate "a rapid decline of the amount of labor," specifically the decline of "mass wage earners" followed by "mass unemployment" as "a process already underway and accelerating" in post-industrial societies. Gorz re-conceptualized what was to be his central notion of "non-class" or "non-workers" as the fulcrum from which to comprehend an entirely new "system of social relations" and associated new social conflict – neither from the perspective of the growing middle classes nor from that of Ronald Inglehart's post-materialism ethos, both of the 1960s and 1970s.

Gorz lays out a dichotomy between those integrated in the social system as mass waged labor, and those to be excluded or expulsed as the mass unemployed. The dividing lines, he argues, are both thin and thick. They are thin because of the unrelenting process of precarization of labor conditions, and the eroding of labor rights historically achieved.

(The) loss of the ability to identify with one's work is tantamount to the disappearance of any sense of belonging to a class...work remains external to the individuals, so does the class being. (p. 67)

They are thick since integration in society is highly dependent on integration in the labor market by means of being able to contribute to a common project which one identifies with or feels part of by means of a job.

Being unemployed or long-term unemployed is a source of marginalization, social stigma, and low esteem. Whereas for Marx the lumpenproletariat were the ones rejected by the industrial societies, Gorz (p. 68) suggests that the "non-class" or "non-workers" are the new marginalized of post-industrialism.

Spanish public opinion reveals: (1) legitimation crises with drastic decline of trust in politicians and in both welfare state and financial services institutions; and (2) social support for the Indignados movement and concern with how the social nature of risk calls for a new social welfare settlement.

Economic stimuli and welfare state social models that were to *embourgeoise* and serve the working class have been undermined:

(1) real wages have not risen in 30 years;

(2) the capability and expectation of starting a conventional family has declined; and

(3) the expectation of buying one's own home has declined. No more "rising tide lifts all boats."

Beyond the Yippies' manipulation of TV news at the end of the 1960s, the Indignados are for Manuel Castells (2012) a post-media movement. In the twenty-first century the explosion of network spaces and the longing for *mutual trust* matter more. There is an eruption of *forums* to discuss common zigzag transversals that require more than government or markets. They require *Social Subjects of Rights*.

There is a sense of a leaderless *rhizomatic revolution* stressing *horizontal power* made more possible by digitized networks than the councils' movements of Rosa Luxemburg or the participatory democracy *groupuscles* of the 1960s (see also Carne Ross, 2013). But these are, Castells argues, also networks of continuing recursive cooperation demonstrating the value of trying new ways of doing things, and not by cramming change down unyielding throats.

Out of the voices of the anti-austerity movements we can discern traces of a social imaginary of novel practices. These are understandable as claims of rightness – with reflexively reconstructable propositional content that can be comprehended as a trajectory – or *arc* – of signifiers. These are signifiers of categorical assertions for a renewal of Social Subject(s) of Rights, a plurality of newer social movements challenging the rule of the algorithm, rather than adhering to some mechanical notion of a Marxian Social Subject. As Claus Offe (2013) notes, the challenge is institutionalizing the open-ended deliberative democracy of the assemblies process of Indignados movements. This amounts to institutionalizing the practice of "listening to respectfully, (and) possibly adopting reasons that others give in open-ended and disciplined face-to-face settings".

But the non-class participating in the Indignados movement is not just well-educated youth adept at social media. Included as well are: (1) other social groups expelled from the system, such as middle-aged professional and civil servants who feel betrayed; and (2) those who never were part of the social system, and never expected to be. The latter are low-skilled working-class youth, among them the NEETs (i.e. "not in education, technology or training") – youth with no work or studies, many thrown out of the construction trades when the real estate bubble burst.

In particular, evident in the Indignados and among their movement leaders are civil servants supporting public education and the health care goals. In one sense, they fight for social rights. In another, they vent their outrage as the years of peaceful cohabitation between the welfare state and capitalism crumble: themselves having been the beneficiaries of professional employment in the welfare state bureaucratic apparatus.

An anxious moment emerges for them as dusk approaches: being fearful that their middle-class expectations are lost. Ironically (that is, dialectically), they are also part of movements of mutual recognition. One mutually recognized prefigurative horizon might be a reciprocal solidarism with the young: a sensed need for some sort of Basic Income allocation or a stakeholder grant upon reaching adulthood.

From the data collected below from CIS (Centro de Investigaciones Sociológicas) surveys in Spain, we can comprehend how the Indignados have the support from the non-class Gorz describes. Further, we are possibly led to conclude that it is mostly (but not only) the fragile so-called middle classes that are the ones undertaking the Indignados movement, and in general protests in Spain. This class would be the non-class Gorz refers to: skilled professionals, civil servants, mass-wage earners, as well as well-educated/well-prepared youth. Their common feature is their lack of expectations in the labor market, based on the basic impoverishment of their living conditions, and the remote possibilities of finding a job.

The non-class or non-workers in post-industrial Spain comprise mostly civil servants, skilled workers in the private sector, and well-educated/well-prepared students. Civil servants need to be thought of as a differentiated group in the middle class, a group that, by and large, has enjoyed privileged working conditions. As the sons and daughters of the welfare state, Gorz noted (p. 56), "bureaucrats guarantee the power of the state without possessing any power themselves. As agents of power or fragments of power, they maintain the mechanisms of domination by enforcing the rules."

Further, wrote Gorz (p. 39), the working-class struggle had been reduced to mass mobilizations designed to bring representatives into power...but not anymore. And:

since the working class can do nothing for itself, it follows the state should do everything for the working class. The seizure of state power by the working class is replaced by the state protection for the working class. Anything lying between the class and the state tends to be abolished. (p. 41)

According to Gorz's book *Farewell* (p. 38), in complex post-industrial societies, work is "heteronomously determined," as a result of the changing functional differentiation of the social division of labor (now a society of transnational networks). Precarization of work and destruction of work are two sides of the same coin. Mass unemployment, Gorz argued (p. 93), would become a predominant feature of post-industrial societies where "people always become anti-human in the name of some inescapable necessity".

In the task of creating public spheres/spaces of autonomy – general assemblies and working cells – Spanish citizens of a young democracy – rich in anarchosyndicalist traditions –

confront:

(1) the intricacies of developing both a collective conscience with the "know-how" to constitute and interact under principles and practices of reciprocal solidarity; or

(2) the creation by the "organized civil society" – with the EU and the World Bank – of some newer corporatist governance, the organized Social Investment State. This is described by Anton Hemerjick (2013) and leaders of the Social Europe movement within the EU and the European Commission.

6

Excursus on Political Corruption and Cronyism in Spain

In recent years, there is also the eruption of political corruption as one of the three main issues that people perceive to be affecting the country. That so much corruption is seen as taking place in the country was noted in qualitative research on the subject two months before the first outbreak of the Indignados movement: "Political Corruption in Spain" – CIS Study #2863 (also see the Spanish online newspaper *Publico.es*: http://www.publico.es/españa/413926/un-gobierno-con-los-lobbies-dentro).

The information collected by this study shows that corruption is socially considered a very serious problem, associated with behaviors of politics and politicians, rather than as a result of the political system *per se*. But it is not viewed as the single problem of the country. Others pointed to the economic crisis, unemployment, or immigration, and these issues equally hold a prominent place in the discourse of citizens.[3]

In that sense, we can speak of the "embodiment of corruption," which damages the image of politicians, but which is not generalized to the political class. Prevailing are feelings of arbitrariness, complicity, impunity, and ultimately helplessness and resignation among the population.

In June 2014 King Juan Carlos abdicates. He is pressured by judicial investigations for his own misuse of government funding for hunting trips in Africa, and of a military rescue helicopter and air transport when he breaks his collarbone while hunting elephants with his German princess-mistress.

Then there are corruption charges of further misuse of public funding by his daughter and son-in-law. The sister of the new King Felipe VI, Princess Cristina, was indicted and tried in 2014/15 for tax fraud and money laundering, making her the first member of the royal family to be tried in court for fraud. In January 2016, she and her husband Iniki Urdangarin – former Olympic handball player and board member of the non-profit consulting firm NÓOS – are tried in court again. NÓOS organizes sports and tourism conferences. Both husband and wife were indicted for skimming off government contracts that they "arranged" to come to NÓOS. As a result, she and her husband are stripped of their titles as Duchess and Duke of Palma. Cristina remains sixth in line to the Spanish throne, a right only she can relinquish.

In September 2014, Isidoro Álvarez dies. He has been the president of "El Corte Inglés," the largest Spanish shopping center. His nephew Ditmas Gimeno succeeds him. Gimeno is linked to the JONS Falange of Primo de Rivera and Franco.

Prime Minister Rajoy's Cabinet includes:

- *Cristóbal Montoro*, Minister of Finance, founder of a major consulting firm that advised companies on how to legally minimize revenue payments to the Spanish Treasury.
- *José Ignacio Wert*, Minister of Education, linked to the Grupo Prisa, which owns the leading publisher of school and university textbooks, and has been an advisor to the BBVA Bank.
- *José Fernández Díaz*, Minister of Home Affairs, who is very close to Opus Dei.
- *Pedro Morenés*, Minister of Defense, formerly Secretary-General of the Association of Businessmen. He was counsel to Instalaza, principal Spanish manufacturer of cluster bombs. He also served as counselor:
  - to MBDA, a large missile manufacturer; as well as
  - to Aritex Cading military design services; I-Sec Iberia security consulting; and Gamo Outdoor, a large American manufacturer of rifles and pistols; part of the executive presidency of Segur Ibérica, a private security corporation;

- *Miguel Arias Cañete,* Minister of Agriculture and Environment, who has large shares and interests:
  - in the petroleum company Ducal SL controlled by his brother;
  - in another petroleum company Canarias, SA; as well as
  - in the Santander and BBVA banks.

  He has chaired the RACE Foundation which encourages the use of automobiles and brick. His wife Micaela Domecq and her family have received funds from the Common Agricultural Policy of the European Union. He has recently been appointed as European Commissioner for Energy and Climate Action.

Further, in September 2014, Emilio Botin, president of the powerful Santander Bank – with many formal and informal interlocks with the commanding heights of Spanish political economy – died at the age of 79 of a heart attack. His daughter Ana Patricia Botin inherited the presidency of Santander Bank. Emilio's last worries reportedly were with the rise of Podemos and the Catalonian and Basque secessionist movements.

In November 2014, Popular Party (PP) Health Minister Ana Mato was forced to step down over corruption charges that she personally profited from her ex-husband's alleged crimes while he was a mayor of a Madrid suburb (Pozuelo de Alarcón). The charges involved allegations of kickbacks for contracts, money laundering, and tax evasion.

By March 2015, three former treasurers of the ruling Popular Party were among 40 indicted (*El Pais*, 26/27 November 2014 and 6 March 2015).

On 15 April 2016, *The Guardian, The New York Times,* and *The Wall Street Journal* report (citing a report in *Confidencial*) that the Panama Papers Scandal has claimed yet another member of Rajoy's Cabinet. This was a scandal reported by the *Süddeutscher Zeitung* of over 11.5 million leaked docuents detailing financial and attorney-client information of the Panamanian law firm Mossack Fonseca, the fouth largest in the world with 600 employees in 42 countries. The allegations were that the law firm's business was primarily in shell companies, tax havens, and off-shoring investments to conceal wealth in places like Jersey, the Seychelles, and the Bahamas. The Minister for Industry, Energy and Tourism, José Manuel Soria, resigned days before he was to appear before the Congress about his links to an offshoring company in the Bahamas. Documents indicate that he was one of two directors of a Jersey-based company called UK Lines Ltd – now called Jersey Mechanical Trading Ltd – dealing with agricultural goods produced from the Canary Islands where he is a local PP leader.

7

The Outraged Grandchildren of the Second Embourgeoisement

The origin and features of the Indignados movement in Spain

In 2008 the economic crisis starts affecting "developed" democracies, but particularly the southern European ones, such as Greece, Italy, Portugal, and Spain, together with Ireland. In the case of Spain, the origin of the crisis can be attributed to three main factors: the "bursting" of the housing bubble in 2008, the financial or banking crisis in 2010, and the fast rise in unemployment taking place since then.

Over its course, the crisis shows its devastating consequences with unstoppable unemployment rates and the generalized impoverishment of the population, affecting not just the working class and the less trained workers from the construction sector (including young people and immigrants).[4] In what has been described as "the new poor,"[5] middle-class professionals working in the private sector with long work experience, or public sector workers[6] in areas such as health, education, or social services, fall into labor instability and uncertainty.

On 15 May 2011 a number of simultaneous demonstrations are held in more than 50 cities in Spain. The movement gains unusual strength, crossing borders, with protests taking place in over 200 European cities and across the Atlantic Ocean in the United States. Shortly after, demonstrations are a feature in more than 800 cities in the world, with the Indignados movement one of the largest.

Social demands of the Indignados were not explicit when the protests started. These protests amount to a recurring "going on" over time in popular assemblies in the squares of hundreds of towns and cities. There is a collective process of configuration and re-configuration in this manifested popular discontent. Further, the absence of clear movement leaders, representatives, or recognizable speakers made it difficult for the media to identify the goals and claims of protesters.

The movement's demands are characterized by its breadth, as well as by its specificity, covering a variety of topics, which can be grouped into two conceptual fields:

(1) *claims on socio-economic and living conditions*, including claims of rights to more efficient and better-quality public services such as health and education, job creation, and the improvement of working conditions, as well as anger at substantial changes in the housing mortgage policies, and alterations in the retirement age; and

(2) *claims related to the functioning of democracy and its institutions, the political system, and political parties*, particularly, the supposed privileges of the political class, the breaking of the so-called dual-party (also called "bipartisan") government between the Socialist Workers Party and the Popular Party, and the calls for more of a sense of popular sovereignty in the political decision-making processes.

The Indignados movement established a close relationship between the two sets of claims, stressing the perversion of democratic principles or the connivance of citizens' representatives with what is identified as "the market" and "big capital" – specifically, the financial sector represented by banks and large multinational companies.[7] There is strong *institutional disaffection* manifest in the social perception that politicians respond to the demands and interests of the "markets" and not to the needs of the population.[8]

The disaffection reveals legitimation crisis – the crisis

of the regime of the Transition State. What is asserted is that the foundations and social experience of democracy are not at all settled. The movement makes common cause with the anti-capitalist, anti-globalization movements and anarchist associations in calling for a transformation in the evolution of the Transition State, specifically in its evolving "democratic consolidation".[9]

Overarching are manifested structural forces: the austerity policies implemented by the European Union, the dismantling of the public sector by means of severe budgetary cuts, and the privatization attempts of public services. Meanwhile millions of euros from the public assets have been transferred for bank bail-outs – amounting to a socialization of banks' losses, and privatization of public assets.[9] Popular outrage at policies of austerity, privatization, and "too big to fail" combine with anger over the high unemployment rates, and the multiple corruption cases coming to light.

The Indignados movement is the result of the *condensation* in space and time of accumulated social claims and outrages over the years; a popular explosion as a consequence of a constant growing discontent with the main regime institutions, and the population's lack of expectations in the near future. There is the bursting of the dam of restraints citizens are able to bear.

As an emergent umbrella movement, the Indignados link with other ongoing social movements engaged in persistent contestation in Spain. One of the clearest examples of the latter is the *Plataforma de Afectados por las Hipotecas* (PAH – Platform for People Affected by Mortgages) which sees itself as the "perfect symbol of inequality and abuse, the boiling crater of the crisis, and on the other hand, a citizen's base movement, whose generous people fight tenaciously to prevent evictions, to change some infamous laws, to demand justice".[10] Its "spokesperson" (disclaiming the role as leader) is Ada Colau. She argues, "I alone am nothing...For there to be truly transformative policy,

71

there needs to be collective processes with the maximum number of people involved".[11]

Madrid had been the epicenter of the Indignados movement. Building alongside PAH, Barcelona emerges as a dual hinge. Barcelona has always been a city which traditionally has a high degree of associative networks voicing social and political concerns. Subsequently they are followed by hundreds of cities. This is the emergent effort at social reinsertion as an intensive struggle against the privatization of regional public health systems, as well as for the reform of the archaic and inefficient education system. Such repercussion sustained a now umbrella intensity once the Indignados movement lost its initial energy.

From the year 2011 to 2015 the number of protests taking up the claims of the Indignados in Spain doubled. Trade unions, together with citizens' associations or work councils, are the most salient social actors promoting these protests. The protests decreased from 2013 to 2015. See Figures 2 to 4.

By 2014, the *Marchas por la Dignidad* (Marches for Dignity) are organized once a month or once every two months, with groups of citizens and a wide variety of associations walking from different parts of the country to gather into a large protest in Madrid. These marches are intended to keep social pressure on political representatives against the austerity measures and in defense of public services and the welfare state. Indignation remains as the persistent sign of collective identity. These sustained massive protests promoted the emergence of hundreds of new associations seeking better social living conditions and stronger standards in Spanish democracy. Results from the May 2014 elections for the European Parliament show how in the Spanish case, left-wing parties – the new Podemos Party and Izquierda Unida – gained strength arguing opposition to austerity policies. What begins is the "electorate's fragmentation" with a severe decrease in the votes for the two main political parties, the Popular Party and the Socialist Party, as both gather under 50% of total votes.

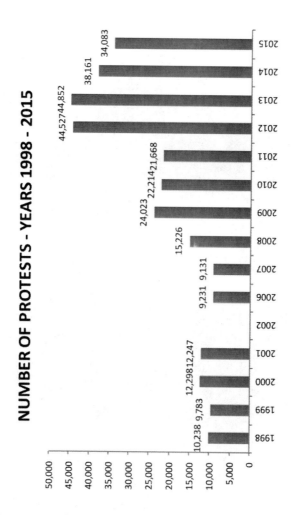

FIGURE 2
Source: Spanish Office for Home Affairs

In that sense, it will soon be worth noting the unexpected
"phenomenon" of Podemos, a party linked to the neighborhood
movements that followed the 15-M, but not defining itself
as the bearer of this movement. Podemos emerges as a new
political party working through a constellation of neighborhood
assemblies or social groups.

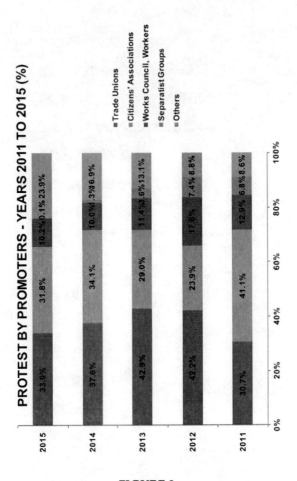

FIGURE 3

Source: Spanish Office for Home Affairs

A popular social movement not linked to political parties and transversing generations, ideologies, and religious orientations

The Indignados denotes a popular movement characterized by: (1) its high social support; (2) its capacity to integrate a wide range of ideologies or religious preferences despite its marked left-wing orientation; and (3) the distance it keeps from political parties and trade unions.

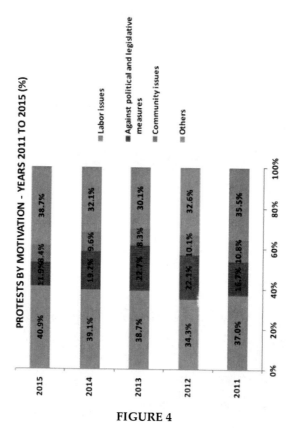

FIGURE 4

Source: Spanish Office for Home Affairs

The survey launched by the Spanish Centro de Investigaciones Sociológicas (CIS) (Research #2905 – June 2011) shows how 50.2% of the population attests to having followed in a "very interested" or "fairly interested" way the mobilizations that took place in May 2011. Further, 70.3% of those who at least have shown some interest describe the actions carried out by the movement as "positive" or "very positive."

In a closer look, results point out that the 15-M protests gained acceptance mostly in municipalities with more than 100,000 inhabitants: almost 67.0% of their population has followed with interest the actions of the movement, and 72.0% rated their actions as positive or very positive.

What do we find when we look at populations with leftist ideology, both in interest in and perception of events (values 1 to 4 in the ideology scale: 77.2% in 1 to 2, and 64.6% at 3 to 4 in interest; 82.7% in 1 to 2, and 83% at 3 to 4 in perception)? Medium- or high-level professionals such as managers and professors, technicians and middle managers, or small businesses (61.8% and 71.7% in interest for the first two cases, 66.3%, 78.7%, and 79.8% respectively in perception). Youth aged 25–34 years old and aged 25–34 (40.0% and 58.0% said they had interest in the protests – 76.1% and 74.8% affirm having a very positive or rather positive opinion on the movement's events). Among students, 62.4% show interest and 83.3% acceptance of the actions promoted.

In other words, the movement is characterized by being primarily urban, with citizens more aware of its importance being left-wing on the ideological scale, skilled professionals, students, and youth (in this case, "young" meaning people up to 34 years old), and widespread among all age groups in what regards acceptance (except for people over 65).

Consequently, ideology, education, and training are relevant variables in explaining social awareness in this case study, as well as social class. The middle and trained classes (again including young people and students) are the core social group supporting the movement. This explains why not just large cities, but also middle-sized towns have been the scenarios of protests, acquiring a significance rarely seen before in the fight for social rights.[12]

Finally, data shows the differences between those *being active followers* in the movement, with a narrower population profile, and those *showing sympathy with it* – exhibiting transversal qualities, especially between age groups or municipality sizes.[13] One of the clues explaining both its mobilizing strength as well as the popular feature of the 15-M protests is the capability the movement has had to achieve the integration not just of the previously mentioned multiple causes and social struggles, but a variety of ideologies and religious orientations, in addition to the intergenerational component.

While the movement has clear leftist voters' support within civil society, so too does it have support: (1) from the social mass of rightist voters disappointed with the course taken by the party currently in power (Partido Popular); and (2) from people without a clear ideological orientation or distant from politics. Similarly, in demonstrations and in the emergent popular assemblies, it was possible to see participants in Catholic movements, together with atheists and agnostics.

The common bonds for a coalition with a degree of solidarity are manifest in the common agreements either expressed or implied in public opinion attestations about the need for substantial changes to ensure certain standards in the living conditions for current and future generations. The prevailing logic is "there is more that unites us than divides us."

The differences between these groups derive from their starting ideological positions as to how to tactically carry out changes or how to identify the means to achieve some viewed horizon. Youth are one of the movement's main bearers of a collective identity; they also act as catalysts. The organization of protests and assemblies has primarily been led by young people; and they are mostly the ones organizing and keeping active debates in the movement's networks based on the Internet.

Social networks on the Internet have played a key role in the start and progress of the movement in initiatives articulated mostly by young people, converging on a common cause: the improvement of people's living and democratic conditions.[14] Digital networks emerge as meeting spaces and dialogue platforms for people with common concerns, for mass identification and discussion of social conflicts. A "digital generation" finds in these networks the horizontal interaction they demand in social and political life. And as such, they become a real political counterpower outside the formal political structures and censorship.

It is important to remark that the 15-M movement is not just constituted by youth. Middle classes, civil servants, or retirees get involved in protests either actively or by giving their support.[15] Youth and adults who face an uncertain future come to share values, perceptions, and feelings, aligning around similar claims.

Finally, despite the sympathetic interest of political parties (particularly left-wing parties) and trade unions, the movement consciously always tried to disengage from them. The parties' and unions' notoriety for hierarchy and leader-based organizational structures seem obsolete for the protesters and their wide range of claims. These are claims pursuing deep institutional and social changes, particularly with an emphasis on more of a shift of sovereignty to the people.

The Indignados movement has emphasized that social experience with democracy is not at all settled, not as yet consolidated. The social perception of politicians is that they respond to the demands and interests of the "markets" and not to the needs of the population, in what has been termed as *political or institutional disaffection*.[16]

The assemblies and camping in the squares: the need to reconquer public discussions and spaces

Undoubtedly the assemblies in the squares of cities are one of the most visible symbols of the 15-M movement and demonstrate efficient strategy in the coherence between its methods or forms of work and its demands.

With public assemblies the Indignados movement raises to the level of "general interest" matters or issues related to far-reaching social conflicts of the country, such as education, health, unemployment, housing, social protection.These topics are discussed in public squares of the cities, in view of any passerby who is able to join them at any time. The assemblies and encampments intend to be the subject of public deliberation and participation. It is understood as a continuous and horizontal participation, where everybody has voice and vote, in transmitting the decentralization message as a critical part of the movement's democratization claims.[17]

In the organization of meetings, a singular and novel working method, one of the hallmarks of the public assemblies, has been the use of sign language when voting for the proposals of participants. This occurs while responding to a practical question, so as not to disturb the neighborhood where and when collective discussions and voting take place.

There is a play on a metaphor related to the citizens with no voice or vote in supposedly democratic societies; related to the citizens not heard by authorities, but finding the means to express themselves, to communicate, and to make decisions through collective dialogue. There is a need for expression and dialogue in a society that does not feel heard by its political representatives; confronting a feeling of powerlessness to the course of events motivates this way of working.[18]

Assemblies have been accompanied by the practice of camping in the central squares; the occupation of the squares by means of camping is one of the most recognizable representions of the Indignados movement. This form of protest also has a high metaphorical strength: the recovery of public space and thus of "the public" by citizens; its use as a meeting space for debate and decision-making on matters of interest to people.

The *Acampada Sol* (camping at Puerta del Sol in Madrid) is set up temporarily (i.e. for a month) like a small city within the city, made of wooden structures and tents, perfectly organized into rooms with different functions (visitor information, attention to the media, catering, leisure, meetings), full of notorious slogans such as "Yes we camp" (in clear reference to Obama's campaign motto "Yes We Can!") and images. This scenario could be been seen around the world.

The Indignados movement raises the recovery of public spaces by the public; of their reconquest following how streets and squares were appropriated by economic, commercial, and institutional or political interests. Its legitimizing assertion is to claim them as meeting points for citizens, for dialogue and collective reflection. Public spaces acquire a symbolic meaning in terms of the reappropriation by citizens of public services and public institutions as a people's right.

Duality and segregation as present in the social structure extends to the disposition of social groups in urban space. Duality is defined by Manuel Castells (1992: 92) as an area of economic growth and high incomes differentiated from that of areas of survival economies, where social mobility between both is scarcely possible. "Social segregation" argues Castells "is the result, and physical barriers correspond to social barriers, ghettos, social and cultural inbreeding, and the invisibility of marginality". For Zygmont Bauman (2008: 57), there is "the trend to abandon public places and retreat to islands...as the main impediment to live with the difference." Others fear the estrangement between people, as fear mediates interpersonal relationships and makes them non-relational, antisociable, and full of cultural anxiety (e.g. Montero, 2008; Martín-Barbero, 2009: 65).

Public spaces in modern cities suffer in the extent of their transformation into private spaces, into semi-public or semi-symbolic entities. For example: the extension of the shopping mall as a model of leisure and consumption; their commodification as consumption style and cost in exchange-value. This consequently restricts the accessibility of public space for certain social groups, and ultimately means the destruction of small tradespeople and their commerce, and thus its sociability.

8

Chronicle of an Explosion Foreseen by Public Opinion

No social scientist anticipated the rise of the popular outrage at Puerta del Sol in May 2011, and with it the start of the Indignados movement in Spain. Yet, the "birth" of this movement could have been foreseen, if more attention had been paid to changes that were taking place before in Spanish public opinion. Particularly, we refer to: (1) the steadily growing distrust of citizens in politics, government, and the economy; and (2) the rupture of bipartisanship. Both patterns show that something was changing in the collective conscience.

The trajectory mentioned above is all gathered from the Spanish State's Centro de Investigaciones Sociológicas (CIS). Survey data over the past 20 years can help us to achieve a better understanding of the social motivations that could have encouraged the Indignados movement. Further, such survey data can show how the claims of this outrage are not the result of improvisation and spontaneity, but stem from the forging – over the last 16 years – of a common consciousness.

First, the 15-M offers a deep critique of the state of the country's politics, its institutions, and the way in which the economy is performing. We can turn to analysis of the trajectory of the public sense of trust in politics, government, and the economy through their corresponding indexes[19] from the year 1996 to 2015. Such analysis leads to two main conclusions:

(1) These three areas of public opinion behave similarly, and act as a whole; thus they need to be analyzed together, along with the evolution of the vote intentions.

(2) There is evidence: of a continuous and increasingly

accentuated discrediting of politics and political parties; of a marked trend of growing negative perception of the government and expectations on the economic situation.

We can show what could represent a change of tendency in the years 2014 and 2015. See Figures 5 and 6.[20]

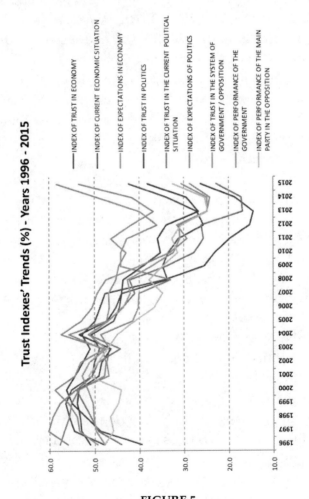

FIGURE 5

Source: Centro de Investigaciones Sociológicas (CIS) – own processing

Public Trust in Economy, Politics and Government (%) - Years 1996 - 2015

GENERAL INDEXES	SPECIFIC INDEXES	1996	1997	1998	1999	2000	2001	2002	2003	2004	2005	2006	2007	2008	2009	2010	2011	2012	2013	2014	2015
INDEX OF TRUST IN ECONOMY	INDEX OF TRUST IN ECONOMY	47.9	54.5	55.6	56.4	55.2	50.5	50.0	48.9	50.7	45.6	44.4	43.9	33.7	34.8	33.6	31.2	25.7	27.1	33.8	42.3
	INDEX OF CURRENT ECONOMIC SITUATION	39.6	46.7	52.0	55.0	56.2	54.4	52.6	51.0	52.8	49.8	48.7	47.7	34.3	25.5	23.1	19.7	15.2	14.4	18.5	26.3
	INDEX OF EXPECTATIONS IN ECONOMY	55.9	60.2	59.2	57.8	54.2	46.7	47.3	46.7	48.6	41.5	40.2	40.1	33.1	44.1	44.0	42.7	36.1	39.9	49.2	58.3
INDEX OF TRUST IN POLITICS	INDEX OF TRUST IN POLITICS	51.0	53.0	53.2	53.8	53.6	49.1	48.4	46.3	53.4	47.1	45.2	43.9	43.6	39.2	35.3	35.9	34.0	28.8	29.4	38.1
	INDEX OF TRUST IN THE CURRENT POLITICAL SITUATION	44.1	49.2	50.8	52.4	54.0	50.5	49.3	44.2	51.2	47.0	43.8	41.1	42.1	34.0	27.8	25.6	28.1	16.7	17.2	22.7
	INDEX OF EXPECTATIONS OF POLITICS	57.7	56.7	55.6	55.2	53.5	47.7	47.5	48.3	55.6	47.2	46.6	46.8	45.2	44.5	42.9	46.3	41.9	36.8	41.7	53.4
INDEX OF TRUST IN GOVERNMENT	INDEX OF TRUST IN THE SYSTEM OF GOVERNMENT / OPPOSITION	47.7	49.7	50.2	50.3	51.4	52.8	51.2	47.4	51.2	47.0	43.6	42.0	42.7	37.4	32.4	31.0	31.1	24.8	24.9	30.6
	INDEX OF PERFORMANCE OF THE GOVERNMENT	48.4	53.4	53.9	55.8	58.8	54.4	53.0	47.7	57.4	52.9	50.4	49.3	47.5	40.1	33.3	29.4	31.5	24.9	24.3	28.6
	INDEX OF PERFORMANCE OF THE MAIN PARTY IN THE OPPOSITION	47.7	45.9	46.4	44.8	44.0	51.2	49.3	47.1	44.9	41.0	36.8	34.8	37.9	34.7	31.5	32.7	30.6	24.6	25.4	32.6

FIGURE 6

Source: Centro de Investigaciones Sociológicas (CIS) – own processing

Second, one of the main criticisms of the 15-M movement is the importance of a bipartisanship: that is, the consensually routine and predictable alternation of power between the two main political parties, the conservative PP and social democrat PSOE, over the entire four decades of post-Franco democratic consolidation. This is reflected in the 2009 vote intentions surveys.

However, with particular intensity between the years 2011 and 2015, PP and PSOE both suffered an unstoppable decline in voting intentions (in 2011 both parties gather 49.1% of the vote intentions; 2012 – 40.6%; 2013 – 27.3%; 2014 – 24.7%; 2015 – 29.2%). See Figures 7 to 10.

On the other hand, the communist Izquierda Unida (IU) has consolidated itself as the most representative left-wing party. In 2013 IU achieves its highest voting intentions rate – 7.5%; and until the strong emergence of Podemos in 2015 – 15.2%. A similar strengthening is seen in the center-right parties as Ciudadanos and UpyD (Unión, Progress and Democracy).

There also emerges a parallel but related unprecedented process which cannot be ignored – the blank ballots and abstentions. Together with the unknown vote, both options add up to: in 2011 – 35.9% of the blank ballots and abstentions; 2012 – 40.8%; 2013 – 51.8%; 2014 – 48.3%; 2015 – 38.0%.

The first explained trend has been labeled as the "crisis of bipartisanship," a drastic decline in the citizens' preference for the "governmental parties" – so called because they are the ones who, by the number of votes they collect, may enter government, compared to other parties, which in any case are classified as "coalition parties." The question is: Whether we can talk of a crisis of this model of alternance in power between two parties, or just a dip (temporary – circumstantial) of the votes achieved by both political forces together? Does this supposed crisis need to be interpreted as a negative phenomenon, or as something positive that results in more diversity, in enrichment of political life, and more political options for citizens? This data shows a clear change in the social preferences with respect to the political arena and parties.[21]

As to the second item of evident data, this is part of what has been recognized in political science as a "crisis of representation":

(1) the citizen's perception that parties currently going along with electoral voting processes do not represent their political or social preferences; and (2) the citizen's "dissatisfaction" with the way the PP and PSOE engage in politics and implement their respective political programs.[22]

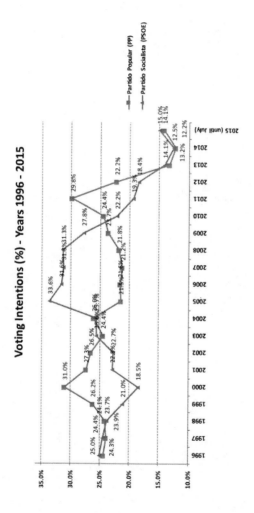

FIGURE 7

Source: Centro de Investigaciones Sociológicas (CIS) – own processing

Both the crisis of bipartisanship and the crisis of representation are important social facts configuring the massive expressions of outrage starting in 2011 and a new period of pacts between traditional and emergent political forces.

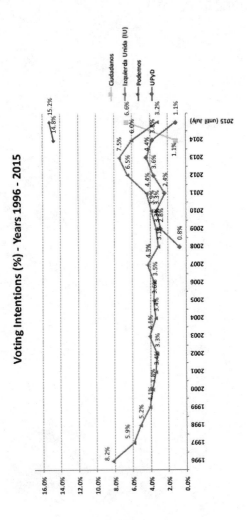

FIGURE 8

Source: Centro de Investigaciones Sociológicas (CIS) – own processing

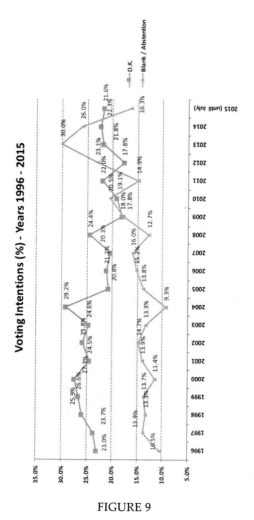

FIGURE 9

Source: Centro de Investigaciones Sociológicas (CIS) – own processing

Third, polls show three sets of problems perceived by society that are an essential aspect of the Indignados movement's demands: (1) unemployment and problems of an economic nature; (2) corruption and fraud, politicians in general, political parties, and politics; and (3) basic public services and public spending regarding the health system, housing, education, and social problems. See Figures 11 and 12.[23]

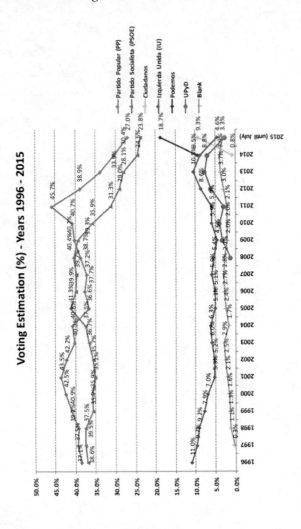

FIGURE 10

Source: Centro de Investigaciones Sociológicas (CIS) – own processing

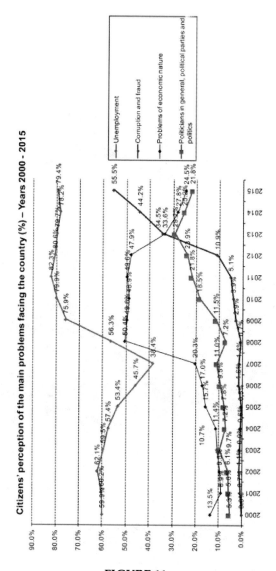

FIGURE 11
Source: Centro de Investigaciones Sociológicas (CIS) – own
processing

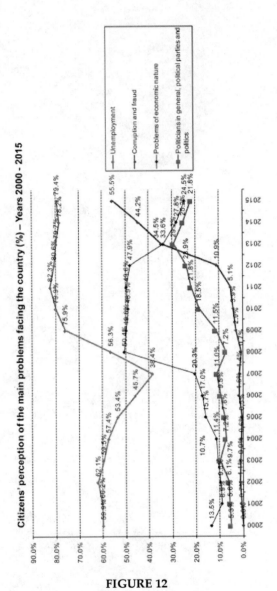

FIGURE 12

Source: Centro de Investigaciones Sociológicas (CIS) – own processing

Finally, we analyze attitudes – and more precisely social discourses – toward political parties, politicians and politics, the current government in power, or the economy, with special attention to the relationship citizens establish between these institutional and social spheres. We do so by reviewing the main conclusions reached by the Centro de Investigaciones Sociológicas (CIS) in Spain in the following three qualitative studies conducted with focus groups and in-depth interviews:

- "Political Representations and 15-M" (CIS – Research #2921 – October and November 2011);
- "The Spanish Discourse on the Relationship between Economics and Politics" (CIS – Research #2865 – February and March 2011);
- "Political Corruption in Spain" (CIS – Research #2863 – March 2011).

The relevance of these studies lies, among other things, in the fact that they were carried out in the months right before and after the coming into being of the 15-M movement in May 2011.

Qualitative studies conducted show how citizens – in an attempt to understand a complex world as some kind of manageable/governable reality – simplify their discourses, reducing them: (1) to a few concepts or notions; (2) to identifiable social actors or fields; or (3) to simple unidirectional relationships between the previous two. Qualitative research is possible here to respond to the "why" of quantitative results.

Political representations and the Indignados movement

The first research mentioned (Research #2921) shows citizens pointing to those considered responsible for the crisis: the local political class, the financial sector, the international arena, and what is verbalized as the "market." Politicians are perceived in prevailing sensibilities and images: those of discredit, mistrust, incompetence, irresponsibility, or lack of will in serving as managers of public assets.

In discourses politicians are represented with arguments such as:

(1) their subordinating themselves to the European governance structures and to the preference they give to the financial sector, the global economy, the "market" representing the "outside";

(2) their inability – and even more their unwillingness – to manage public affairs in order to effectively surmount the crisis, by developing effective policies, which primarily will prioritize the need to counter the deteriorating living conditions of the population;

(3) their inherent corruption as a general attribute of politicians; and

(4) the privileges enjoyed by the political class, which most of the population do not have access to.

In this last regard, the privileges attributed to politicians – e.g. high salaries, the daily amenities of office-holding, legal immunities to certain legal situations – contribute to the social construction of their image as the "political class" (*La Casta*). That political class is perceived by those outside it as having its own values and lifestyle; but above all, having class interests that would always protect it against other classes' interests, such as citizens in general. The political class is perceived as remembering citizens only at election time. Similarly, this research shows perceptions of how politicians, as a result of their "social distance" from citizens, are tempted into corrupted behaviors and a lack of interest in citizens – the citizens whom it is their mandate to represent.

In particular, the research reveals two central issues: (1) to make possible a greater plurality in political parties offering alternatives to the traditional parties, and proposing changes in the electoral system; and (2) to emphasize the fight against corruption as one of the major "ills" of the emergent consolidated democracy.

Finally, results show two main discourses on the 15-M movement. On the one hand, the Indignados are appreciated for being a horizontally democratic movement, heterogeneous, young, peaceful, apolitical, and essentially left-wing with innovative proposals. This movement is appreciated for having managed: (1) to stir consciences and to create uncertainty among the political class; and (2) to put firmly on the public agenda important issues such as the housing problem, or the shortcomings of the electoral system, among others.

On the other hand, dismissive discourses: (1) qualify the movement as illegal in some of its actions, such as the occupation of city-center plazas; (2) brush aside the movement as inherently "anti-system" in spirit, utopian, and with romantic traits; (3) cannot comprehend the legitimation claims and arguments for the start of the movement. With regard to this lack of comprehending, 15-M is criticized for not having either clear objectives or clear organization, thus foreshadowing/prefiguring ineffective attempts to achieve its goals. There is shared cautious uncertainty, or lack of confidence regarding the continuity of the Indignados over time in maintaining the intensity of proposals and notoriety in the media. Can the Indignados establish a durable presence?

The relationship between economics and policy

The Indignados stirred popular concern and access to concepts, ideas, and approaches on economics, with the media as the main platform for all. This is probably one of the main contributions of the Indignados movement to Spanish society, as it has survived in time.[24]

Increasing social criticism of political parties and politicians, or of their inability to manage the economic crisis, motivates another qualitative study conducted two months before the massive 15-M protests started, titled "The Spanish Discourse on the Relationship between Economics and Politics" (CIS Study #2865). That study aimed at understanding how the population argues the relationship or interaction between economics and politics.

The analysis of the information gathered once more points to the persistence of social discourses: (1) where politics is seen as subordinate to the "economic powers" and, moreover, working for the interests of "the market"; and (2) where economic phenomena are understood as acting in an autonomous way, seriously damaging civil society. Citizens are understood as having lost any capability to take effective control over economic events through their political representatives.

The Spanish economy is imagined as dependent, unproductive, fragile, and unstable, and not well integrated into the overall European economy. The minimum functions of policy to steer the economy, such as monitoring, supervising, or controlling through regulation, are perceived as limited and implemented only in urgent situations. For example, when consequences for society are irreversible, and with a perspective distant from the needs of the citizenry. The government appears to be responsible for seeming to be complicitly abetting an attitude of lack of initiative and control to prevent or manage the crisis for the people inside Spain, complying with interrelated exogenous forces of the Troika of the IMF, ECB, and the European Commission (forces outside which Spain acceded to).

There is a sense of betrayal by the ruling party – at the time the PSOE. This is highly present in the survey research, indicating a tendency to turn against PSOE and to vote for the opposition PP. At the same time, ideological identifications water down and thin out explanations of the nature of the crisis. In that light, maybe one of the experiences achieving highest approval has been the work of the *Plataforma de Afectados por la Hipoteca* (PAH

– Platform for People Affected by Mortgages). This association has not only stopped hundreds of mortgages, but has been able to introduce partial changes in the law on mortgages in Spain. The social was re-embedded/reinserted beyond the capabilities of the political class.[25]

9

Horizontal Democracy: Rhizomic Social Movements of Indignation

Rhizomic social movements of indignation

Indignez-vous! (2010) by Stéphane Hessel anticipates the outrage of a lost generation – as the becomingness of a generalized condition (Ainger, 2013). The forms and spaces created by the Indignados movement, questioning regime legitimacy and acquiesced-in austerity policies, shock and provoke. Yet, they also try to anticipate new policy practices: specifically, institutionalizing new policy directions in employment relations, skill formation, and social relations in the wake of innovation and obsolescence in labor markets and both higher education and its financing.

The *Indignez-vous* movements that Hessel anticipated represent a different mode of student countercultural movement than their 1968 predecessors. These anti-austerity movements are not just the new social movements spurred by the legitimation crises of the welfare state that Jürgen Habermas, Claus Offe, and Alain Touraine described in the 1970s and 1980s.

In particular, the Indignados are a spatially oriented movement, a coalescing assemblage of horizontal power. They do so with immanent forms of track switching policy-wise, of de-coupling and re-coupling. They are a new species of social movement anticipated by Alain Touraine and his student Manuel Castells – operating as switchers controlling the connections between networks, embedded in the communication process.

While relatively inexpensive public higher education is at the combative edge of today's youth revolt, it is more than a student phenomenon. It is a struggle of the young to enhance and transform social commitment to public higher education and to employment as pillars of a welfare state that must adapt to a revolution in spatiality and scalarity that is the consequence of the functional differentiation of labor markets associated with globalization.

Today's youth revolt: (1) rails against the monetarization of humanity; (2) senses that young people are falling outside a decomposing socio-economic order into a whirlpool of debt bondage and suffocation; and (3) expresses a feeling that that they are caught between a welfare state calcified into an ancient regime oriented toward income protection, and a needed order of improved labor market participation.

The revolt takes on the character of a movement of "autonomism" and horizontality: organized spontaneously as a parallel universe outside and separate from "power structures." The revolt does not just wait for "the deal" proffered by policy technocrats, but demands alliances on its own terms.

This moves Manuel Castells in his recent *Networks of Outrage and Hope* (2012) to refer to this assemblage of new social movements as "rhizomatic" movements of indignation. They are rhizomatic in their horizontality of underbrush beneath the surface that sends out myriad shoots from its nodes that give rise to a new plant. Rhizomatic movement is the epoch-defining metaphor defined by Gilles Deleuze (1968, 1988; and Deleuze and Guattari, 1987) as the myriad enfolding and unfolding of plurality (1) that cannot be comprehended arborescently, or (2) as a unity that occurs when the stem begins to split and the root begins to wither.

In reflecting on the Occupy Movements of 2011 and 2012, Marianne Maeckelbergh (2012) emphasizes the main underlying current of *horizontality* as both a value and a practice, as:

- a transversing of fields;
- a creating of new socially differentiated forms of lived and imagined public space; and

- a pooling of common intensities.

Linking the *encuentros* of the Zapatistas in the middle 1990s, Maeckelbergh notes that within these movements is a distinctive affective and practical impulse to horizontality. This is an impetus to decentralized horizontal decision-making aimed not at making universally binding decisions, but at creating and facilitating networks of communication and resistance. Networks are constituted to help people organize against the neoliberal norms, subjectivities, and practices of a globalized epoch of capitalism, and the post-2008 crisis austerity cutbacks that follow.

In Spain, barter networks and local currencies have emerged, as the *Plataforma contra los Desahaucios* (PAH) and the citizens' assemblies in neighborhoods help residents with foreclosure/housing issues. Further, three protest movements overlap, interpenetrate, and reinforce the Indignados: *marea blanca* (white tide) in defense of public health care; *marea verde* (green tide) in defense of public education; *marea violeta* (violet tide) against the recently approved most restrictive European Union law on abortion.[26]

It is the mutually recognized needs emergent in the hard living conditions that lead to these experiences of mutual solidarity. Survival-oriented, for many there seem no other ways out. These newly created mediations help in the realization that solutions won't come from the authorities.

Rather than assuming that equality can be declared or created through a centralized authority that is legitimated to rule by "the people", moral practices of horizontality rest on the assumption that inequality will always permeate (for) ever social interaction. This shift in assumptions results in an acknowledgement that these inequalities always exist and that each person is responsible for continuously challenging these inequalities at every step of a decision-making process. (Maeckelbergh, 2012: 211)

These *Indignez-vous* movements have emphasized transformatory process rather than just practice in confronting the gap separating the potential from the actual. It is a process that projects and prefigures a new sense of binding-ness, a new sense of social bond providing the glue to hold a new sense of solidarity together. Not a reversion to what Emile Durkheim denoted as a communal mechanical solidarity of resemblance. But neither is it some functionalist integration of interdependent roles imagined as an organic solidarity. Durkheim himself saw industrial society at the turn of the twentieth century *in medias res*, in a continuing transitory segmental solidarity. The narrative is no longer understood as some universalizing modernist grand narrative. The movements of *Indignez-vous* of 2011/12 prefigure and reflect socio-economic dynamics toward a reciprocal solidarity confronting the possible lost generations of young people saddled with insufficient work possibilities and debt.

The world is rhizome, not arborescence. Unlike trees and the verticality of their roots, the rhizome connects many points laterally/horizontally to other points. Here we include connections *between* people (actors) and machines/technologies/texts (actants).

There is what Henri Lefebvre (1974, 1980) referred to as "an explosion of space." Lefebvre conceives of a social-spatial dialectic. Space is impermanent, and not a pre-given configuration. It is neither a "subject" nor an "object," but rather a set of relations and forms. Space is the embodiment and medium of social relations. Social life is understandable as both space-forming and space contingent. It accounts for representational space and representations of, as well as for, their interrelationships and their links with social practice. Social relations of class can be "reconfigured and possibly transformed through the evolving spatiality which makes them concrete" (Soja, 1989: 127). Social and spatial practices intersect, and are dynamic and mutable in terms of producing new meanings – new postmodern geographies as Soja calls them – that enter into a society's transformation.

Space is constantly being reordered into various hybrid connections in interurban, interregional, inter-ethnic conurbations – vertically, horizontally, diagonally, centrifugally, centripetally, spherically, and fractally.

The "real space" of traditional geography is replaced by a space that is articulated within and between networks with origin in society. It is a space defined by connectivity of nested levels of scale deployed in the attempted coordination of obligations among mutually connected actors attempting to act as reciprocators in coping with the risk and sustainability of these very networks.

The rhizomic moving trajectory cannot be reduced to any sort of fixed constellation of unities. Everything that exists only becomes and never is. This is an ontology of becoming without being, emphasizing movement and flow, de-coupling and re-coupling. In *Creative Evolution* (1911) – a spur to the thinking of Gilles Deleuze (1966) – Henri Bergson noted that the disrupting movement of novelty always involves "living penetration," not derived relationships between discrete points or positions in space, not some fixed subject position in some fixed constellation.

The focus is not on the surfaces, but on the fibrous and stringy-like nature of rhizomes and networks, and on the nodes that emerge with as many dimensions as they have connections. Actors are not conceived as fixed entities but as flows, as circulations, objects undergoing constant trials within the circuitry and nodes of globalizing processes.

This is an actor-rhizome ontology of cascading emergent connection and reconnection. Life is understood as hidden in rhizome, spinning off seeds within available fissures: ceaselessly establishing connections, junctions, interconnections – a woven and rewoven meshwork. The focus is on the upsurging wanderings of rhizomes as they incessantly disrupt everyday ways of making sense and generating new "forms of life." In comprehending the rhizomic wanderings that constitute the emergence of creativity and novelty, we grasp fugitive flashes of ethical moments haunting the present with strong durational intensity that test and shatter force fields of bounded rationality.

After four decades of focus on externalities – the unintended consequences of purposive collective action – we have reached the other far shore. This is the recognition of the side effects of rhizomes in adaptive processes that accidentally sustain life. Path-dependency approaches provide endogenous models of how contingent events set into motion patterned chain events that have determinist properties. This explains how we compliantly get "locked in" into the sequential "institutional stickiness" of seeing optimal practices. Order is understood as the synchronic expected emergence of reproduced practice. Novelty – as in path disrupting and path creating – can be understood as diachronic emergence.

Policy-making and policy-implementing regimes can be comprehended as riddled with a meshwork of rhizomic networks and subnetworks. The focus is on zigzagging/transversal diachronic path-creating action rather than on seemingly determined/sequenced synchronic path-dependent behavior. Diachronic and transversal emergences involve breaking free from our histories: disrupting, rupturing, and triggering the creation of new meaning. An ontological "becomingness" comes to phenomenologically supervene as new collective cognitive and experiential properties.

The embeddedness of bounded rationalities is transgressed. The homeostatic resilience and recuperative power of systemic negative feedback loops are overcome. Creative acts of intuition, cognition, and interpretation meaningfully navigate the tangle, mangle, and flow of assemblages even as they constitute them. Path creation is understood as practices of "mindful deviation" by boundary spanners, entrepreneurs, and network reciprocators in surpassing the seeming logical sequentialism of the suboptimal inert, the cluttering clichés, and the absurd (Garud and Karnøe, 2001).

In the current context of socio-economic crisis, civic networks based on solidarity and self-help values and mutuality have multiplied in Spain. These initiatives might not be as notorious as social protests that take place in the streets, but they represent a clear example of how civil society is able to organize to face the fast impoverishment of their living conditions.

For example, people in towns and cities all over the country have joint access to the so-called "social coin" and to the "banks of time."[27] In the first case, by means of networks of entities and cooperatives, whose aim is to activate local commerce and markets under pressure from the predominance of multinational firms and the current economic crisis, or consolidate ethical financial products by means of a "real economy," on social and democratic principles. Equally, banks of time work as barter networks based on solidarity principles that make it possible for a population with low incomes to have access to basic services or needs.

10

Precarity: Indignation as Anti-Austerity/ Anti-Neoliberalism Movements

As the pillars of the policy regimes of social democracy implode, we realize that society is constructed, and that the seeming stable surfaces and veneers of solidity, solidarity, and civility are dissolvable. Rhizomatic indignation manifests fugitive flashes, fugitive differences, fugitive emergent moments transversing the force field, attempting to shatter it, before they sublimate into solidity and solidarity. These fugitive flashes remind us how so many of us are Indignados nowadays.

These fugitive differences are bearers of mutually recognizable signifiers and commitments. Bearers of a fugitive intersubjectivity wherein we mutually recognize each other:

- as intentional agents in moments of creative juxtaposition: moments of the collage/montage of becoming;
- as bearers of a fugitive yet prophetic minority impelling us, plunging us into self-reflexive valuation and revaluation, disrupting promises of reflexive global governance.

Social rights as human rights are back on the agenda. J.M. Bernstein (2001) refers to these as flashes of "fugitive ethical moments" that haunt the present as they rupture it out of time in a not wholly cognitive manner – with strong durational intensity, offering multiple temporalities in a way foreshadowed by Bergson and Georges Sorel.

With the dismantling of the 1945–75 social democratic regimes, we have plunged into a Latour-like world where governance is more understood in association(s) than in sovereignty. These are associations with multiple centers, sites, and nodes – the society

103

of networks. As Jacques Donzelot (1984) and Niklas Rose (1999; cf. Rose and Miller, 2008) show, this is a world where the state no longer positions itself as a manager that can solve society's problems, but deflects these problems back on society. Can protests and resistance stem the tide of liquidation, destruction, and austerity unleashed by the economic crisis? Can they initiate tides of their own – tides of social re-embeddedness/ social reinsertion?

Political economy is not a morality play; it is instead rooted in regulative governance rationales. The Indignados are buffeted by more than the forces of globalization. They are swallowed up in the whirlpool of illusions of "expansionary austerity": growth based on cutbacks (Blyth, 2013), suffocated by illusions of eventual equilibrating, while the bailed-out banks are allowed to continue to regulate themselves.

Can we pose a supply-side social democracy to counter the predominant supply-side neoliberalism? (See Streeck, 1992, 2012, 2014; Streeck and Schäfer, 2013.) Along with the deregulation of capital, there is a normative re-regulation wherein *risks* become de-socialized, privatized, and individualized. This is a neoliberal cultural counter-revolution – a counter-legitimatory rationale with a constituted normative valence that infects the desire and affinities within which we live.

Globalized neoliberalism generates a class fragmentation in its dismantling of social insurance programs. This is a social class of frustrated educated youth without predictability, without security, and with a restricted range of social rights. They live in a context of increasing temporary agency labor, outsourcing, and abandonment of non-wage benefits by firms. They live, in the words of Guy Standing (2012), "bits and pieces lives," in and out of jobs without a narrative of occupational development, precariously insecure.

Standing (2011) – working out of the Decent Jobs Project of the International Labor Organization – refers to these as *the*

Precariat, and delineates the new social strata of the advanced societies of the developed world as follows:

- *the Elite;*
- *the Salariat;*
- *the Proficians* with bundles of skills, who live opportunistically with their wits and contacts;
- *the Proletariat;*
- *the Precariat;*
- *the UnderClass* or the lumpenproletariat, often living in gangs and involved in addictions.

The Precariat is cut off from:

- classic circuits of capital accumulation;
- the institution of collective bargaining;
- fixed workplaces that were the pillars of twentieth-century social democracy; and
- the working-class parties allied with welfare state policies.

Frustrated educated youth face a drift into: (1) the infantilization of limitless electronic game play, streamed popular entertainment, and passive use of time in front of electronic screens; (2) part-time, flex, temp and freelance work; and (3) worse, a drift into the lumpenproletariat in an underground of illicit jobs.

The term *précarité* – as in *travail précare* – emerged in France during the 1980s in socio-economic literature with the emergence of the neoliberal regime of capital accumulation to characterize the changing patterns of work and declining centrality of the wage relationship in structuring society that Gorz had pointed out.

The Precariat is a stratum, not a class-in-formation: not a class-for-itself; not a class posed in a relational manner; not a part of a transformation aimed at overcoming the "realm of necessity." It is a non-class in Gorz's terminology, used as an expansion of the reserve "army of labor" to discipline the labor market. Marginal and underemployed, the Precariat – very much the new graduates who are underemployed or unemployed – represents a newer incarnation of what Karl Marx and Nicos Poulantzas referred to as petty bourgeoisie falling into the stratum of lumpenproletariat.

Neoliberal normative valence involves an explicit imposition on the political, cultural, and social systems by a particular market rationality that inverts the force upon the economic agent by the sympathetic moral sentiments posited by Adam Smith and the Scottish Enlightenment. Actor-network theory (ANT) scholars Koray Calisken_and Michel Callon (2009) label this as "economization." It involves what Latour describes as a new form inserted in network nodes for "ruling spaces at a distance." This is a system of rule operating in an extremely fluid mode: less rooted in the material practices of institution, and more oriented to processes of rules (see Walters, 2004). Aihwa Ong (2006, 2007) sees all this as less a unified hegemonic order of policies than a fluid process of rule involving "migratory mobile technologies":

- for self-mastery so as to secure optimal profits; and
- for discerning points of entry into non-hierarchical/ even heterarchical network flows so as to cash in on asymmetrically unfolding job opportunities.

In summing up, neoliberal normative valence involves: (1) an emphasis on the capability for individual self-care and self-investment; (2) a dematerializing and deregulating of labor so as to expose labor to a more flexible and precarious contracting process; and (3) technologies of calculative performance within the polymorphous perversity of assessment audits that make Taylorist scientific management monitoring seem kind and helpful.

11

Emergent Alternative Political Parties: Podemos...and Then On to Barcelona en Comú

Podemos (We Can!), *Ahora Madrid* (Madrid Right Now), *Ganemos* (Let's Win) and then on to *Barcelona en Comú* (Barcelona in Common)
What forges the anteroom for the Spanish Indignados?

• The economic crisis starting in 2008 and the subsequent widespread dismissals in a country traditionally with one of the highest unemployment rates in Europe.

• The imposition of a wide range of unpopular austerity measures based on severe budgetary cuts on public services, along with the corruption cases transversing most political orientations and institutions.

With the coming to power of the conservative Partido Popular a month after the protests arose (June 2011), there was a feeling of an absence of visible, tangible, or immediate relevant "results" or influence of the movement to generate change. There was a sense that 15-M was a spontaneous outrage with no continuity in time or sustained strength: of a failed movement.

The Indignados continued to stand for protest against the passiveness or inaction of the Socialist Party in face of evidence of: (1) the bubble burst in the construction sector, and (2) the crashing down of the financial sector prior to the start of the economic crisis in 2008. Political disaffection and the intensity of protests continued in the period following the general election of 2011, against the austerity measures and subsequent further deterioration in the population's living conditions under the Partido Popular regime of Prime Minister Rajoy. This is the prelude to the downfall of the Spanish two-party model. Startling results in the elections for the European Parliament come in May 2014. The vote brought *Podemos* (Yes We Can!) firmly into the political arena. A total of 1.2 million votes (five deputies) go to a party created just four months before the polls. Podemos is a political project under construction, barely with any formal structure or political program, and counting on a scarce budget of 120,000 euros. Once again, we have a surprising new movement actor, shaking the political order in a manner not really foreseen even in polls leading up to the election.

Three months later, Podemos is the second political force in polling the "direct intention vote," and the third after the application of statistical corrections in survey responses. This amounts to a doubling of the votes gathered in the elections to the European Parliament, and surpassing the communist Izquierda Unida. Soon, Podemos is the political party with the highest presence on the social media/Internet. An emptiness in political life creates a window of opportunity for emergent initiatives. Official disregard and belittling response toward protesters reaches a turning point with a project like Podemos suddenly breaking into the formal structures of the political system.

A project that started from below, at the neglected margins of society, without much social visibility and recognition, enters into forums of institutionalized decision-making. The Indignados showed that they are a movement in it for the long haul and not just a spontaneous outrage of a clearly durable time-spanning citizen disaffection with politics, politicians, and the current economic trends. It manifests that it is a movement that keeps the mobilizations alive by making the leap from the negative agenda based on what it is against, to developing an electoral program sustaining specific proposals aspiring to and intending deep transformations.

In this section we will focus on Podemos as an experimental and creative sociopolitical project: how it organizes, the clues for achieving high media notoriety, the perspectives and strategies for the next local elections in 2015, and finally the birth of *Ganemos* (Let's Win), a coalition platform for political alternatives.

Podemos, a novel sociopolitical project

In the European context, we recently witnessed both frustrated initiatives, such as, in France, the *Nouveau Parti anticapitaliste* (NPA, associated with Olivier Becancenot), in Italy *Movimento 5 Stelle* (M5S – the Five Star Movement of Beppe Grillo), and successful political projects such as *Syriza* in Greece.

Podemos starts as a spinoff project led by Pablo Iglesias (35 years old in 2014), an experienced and skilled spokesman, together with a group of other professors *at the Faculty of Sociology and Political Science and Sociology at Universidad Complutense in Madrid. The economic and institutional crisis represented an opportunity to promote a totally new sociopolitical alternative (see Pictures 1 and 2).*

PICTURE 1
Podemos presentation in Madrid – Pablo Iglesias – 16 January 2014
Courtesy: Podemos

PICTURE 2
Podemos presentation in Madrid – Iñigo Errejón and Pablo Iglesias –
16 January 2014
Courtesy: Podemos

Podemos' approach to politics and to political practices pivots on the core idea of "people's empowerment." Only when people become empowered can it be said they are citizens with full rights. The theme is to tactically enable a collectively empowered movement, as "social majorities" take control of institutions and the decision-making processes. The priority is not seizing the power but surrounding it through community movement organizations pursuing "empowerment." The former would be the necessary condition for the viability and sustainability in time of the latter; a sociopolitical majority is the previous stage to the electoral majority and the re-emergence of a "new democracy," a "twenty-first-century democracy."

The progressive "conquering of sociopolitical spaces" involves the promotion, building, multiplication, and consolidation of "spaces of empowerment," their synchronization into a univocal voice, while joining the already institutionalized ones, ongoing for years. These spaces take the particular form of popular assemblies spreading out all over the territory, structured by collective debates engendering horizontal social interaction. This involves the occupation and collective re-signification of public spaces with experimental experiential new ways and forms of discussion on shared concerns – the collective construction of a social agenda to reinsert and re-embed into an institutionalized politics that has been denying such a social agenda. In sum, a "new way" of doing politics: experimental, from below.

Under this approach, people engage and experience politics by "doing politics," a shift from the passive welfarism of a now inert social democracy. There, citizens are called to participate in politics only during electoral processes. The shift is toward direct and continuous participation, consultation, and accountability.

The social class conflicts and struggles in Marxist terms are avoided, and the clash is presented between the people and *La Casta*: a central *floating signifier* – to use the language of Ernesto Laclau – emerges in Podemos' discourse.

Thus, the dichotomy is presented as one pitting the real politics and real democracy, for the people and by the people, against the embedded politics of the elites and for the elites. What is posed is the will of the "social majority" over that of the "privileged minority." The strategy is to plan and design the implementation of novel effective channels and practices for social participation, as the democratization of Spanish politics.

This discourse finds its historical anchoring in the current Constitution of 1978, designed in the transition from Franco's regime to a form of democracy. According to Podemos, the Catalan movement Guanyem Barcelona, left-wing secessionist parties, or the communist Izquierda Unida, the current Constitution is the result of the elites' pacts that effectively excluded a design for popular sovereignty.

In what has been termed as the "political culture from the Transition," the oligarchic democracy (including the monarchy) would need to be replaced by new "social pacts" built from the "social bases." These decentered social pacts interlink the new society. The reforms within the Constitution of 1978 would then be the key to create a totally new state, a "constituent process" leading to the "constituent power" resting in the people; not a second Transition, but a democratic rupture.

Podemos' internal organization and structure

Podemos is designed as an assembly-based party, horizontality its main organizational principle. It develops in 2014 as "a formation with an open strategy" and in this sense as a provisional project, until the conclusion of its planned "foundational assembly" at Vistalegre in the autumn of 2014.

There affiliates will define the organizational structure and political program of Podemos through a discussion process on an "organizational document" draft. It is intended as an organization aiming from its genesis at a distinctive identity based upon high levels of internal democracy and transparency: on citizens leading the decision-making processes and involved in "doing politics."

All affiliates have the right: to the direct election and revocation of responsibilities in the organization; to participate in debates; to participate in drafting the electoral programs or designing their candidates' lists; to the principle of an equal vote's value; and to vote in all important relevant decisions.

According to its initial provisional "organizational document," Podemos organizes with a basic structure consisting of a spokeswoman or "chorus of spokesmen," a board, a citizens' council, a commission of rights and guarantees, and the "circles" (*circulos*, or local assemblies). With an organizational group comprising 10 to 15 leaders, the circles are the main vehicle for political debate, the basic structure and core salient organ in the interaction with citizens, in charge of conciliating the shared objectives with the diversity of sensibilities.

The circles are structured both on territorial and on sectorial bases. The intention is to provide wide autonomy in the ways these circles want to work on their own and in horizontal relations with other circles. These would be the spaces where decentered community feelings and social bonding emerge, and move toward a regional and national Confluence.

Citizens' assemblies have the task of electing a citizens' council with open lists. This is for a citizens' council with a spokeswoman or "chorus of spokesmen." It is in the circles where the main decision-making body is constituted at the municipality level. *Do strength,* an added value to traditional ways of *doing politics.*

Equally, new technologies play a crucial role in Podemos. Since 2008 when Barack Obama started the 2.0 politics, political parties can't ignore communication with citizens based on the Internet, and especially those starting a new political project. In this regard, the high mobilization capacity in the social media is one of the clues for Podemos' success. Pablo Iglesias and his close comrades have relied for years on the Internet for the diffusion of debates on sociopolitical issues. Developing platforms such as "La Tuerka," "Fort Apache," "Plaza Podemos," "Agora Voting," or "Democratic Laboratory," their aim is to approach debates among the people in a bidirectional communication process, with citizens feeling an integrative and proactive part of the discussion process.

At this early developmental stage, Podemos as *formación* is committed to making use of display assemblies – by *streaming,* and by coordinating the voting process both by personal attendance and through online participation. The process of affiliation can also be done online. These initiatives contributed to the achievement of high affiliation rates in a short time period. As did two other distinctive organizational features: (1) there is no economic contribution required for affiliates; and (2) there is no sense of incompatibility/inconsistency with being part of a different political party.

In sum, Podemos combines the assembly model with a basic organizational structure and new technologies based on the Internet. Nevertheless, its "dual structure", which combines different degrees of peripheral autonomy with management and leadership from the center, would become a source of contradictions: especially with regard to the excessive influence of the leaders or the leading group in the decision-making processes, where assemblies and thus citizens or the people would not necessarily "have the last word."

Podemos and the media

As noted above, Podemos engages in novel communication means and messages in the social media. But likewise it uses TV as well. Both are important factors in its success and popularity. Relying on its leader Pablo Iglesias and a team of experts in new technologies, the communication campaign designed for the May 2014 elections to the European Parliament was highly rated comparatively, having achieved 33.6% acceptance.[28] See Figure 13.

During the pre-electoral campaign and straight on down until today, Podemos spokepersons have drawn the attention and support from *La Sexta* TV Channel, which is part of the media group Mediapro. This is a media network with a conservative orientation, but broadcasting programs focusing on social issues; and a network that has been giving high support to Podemos' spokespersons, even when they were scarcely known. In times of financial vulnerability and extremely high competition in the communication sector, the logic followed is "business is first, ideologies come after."

Mediapro leads audience ratings, finding in social discontent a source of significant and sustaining TV viewers. Though Spanish media is highly controlled by conservative and Catholic interest groups, dissident voices on the current state of politics

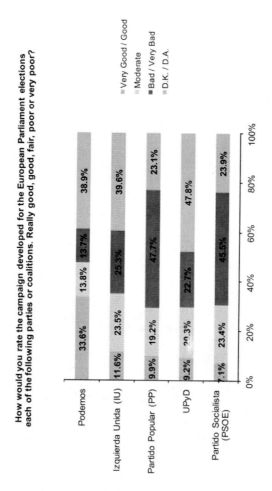

FIGURE 13

Source: Centro de Investigaciones Sociológicas (CIS) – own
processing

unexpectedly found in this media group an opened window to
express and communicate with society. They found the necessary
jump from the Internet-based communication channels to the
traditional televisual mass media.

The following are some of the featured aspects of Podemos'
communication strategy. Podemos mostly focuses on social

discontent as indicated in quantitatively based socio-economic trends. They spotlight severe problems present in the country, such as the increasing high poverty rates, uncontrolled unemployment, cuts on public services, corruption, the rolling back on labor rights.

Their style of framing arguments is frequently labeled by other parties as *populism* – "saying the things people want to hear." In this form of discourse the term "La Casta" is recurrent, alluding to the differences in the living condition, status, and power between the population as a whole and a privileged elite, and triggering a debate on its suitability.

The inefficiency of the two larger political parties is also a topic of discussion. The two-party model is the main target.

Podemos' communication strategy has, as its purpose, endeavoring to be coherent in its means and principles and the building of a critical and conscious citizenship. There is a concerted effort to avoid the predominant style of political commentary that is the norm in the mainstream media. There the *modus vivendi* is one that is based on confrontation and mutual discrediting. It is a style that is devoid of content. Furthermore, it is a style where core economic, political, and social issues are dealt with superficially – where they are dealt with in a casuistic tone.

Particularly, the Podemos communication strategy is based on the stresses of contradictions present in the discourses of both the socialist and conservative parties. The criticism of the PSOE focuses on their detachment from the redistribution discourse, showing complicity in the so-called *La Casta*. The PP is portrayed as being in contradiction in presenting itself as a liberal party – when it is only oriented to an economic liberalization that gives up sovereignty to the IMF and EU or other external power decision-centers. Personal sacrifices are promised and fulfilled – like not accepting a salary as an MEP (a deputy at the European Parliament) that would exceed three times the minimum wage.

Such promise has been a core part of the communication strategy.

Podemos voters' profile

To outline the socio-economic profile of its voters, we once more draw upon the Spanish Centro de Investigaciones Sociológicas (CIS).[29]

Results based on the labor category (see Figures 14 to 19) show how the Podemos voters' profile is mainly shaped, in order of importance, by the unemployed (19.2% from all who have worked before or looking for their first job); those non-classifiable in the labour market (17.7%); and students and unskilled workers (17.3% and 17.0% shares respectively).

As 2014–15 proceeded, there was little acceptance of the predominant norms of socio-economic practices in segments that have traditionally been followers of the two main parties, such as:

- those in unpaid domestic work, mostly linked to the immigrant working-force (6.1%);
- retirees and pensioners (6.8%);
- businesspeople with employees;
- high-ranking civil servants;
- senior executives and self-employed professionals (7.6%); and
- farmers living in the countryside (9.1%).

In that sense, the data also suggests that Podemos is the second preferred party among traders and small businesses (13.2%), and gathers similar voting shares to the main political parties from professionals and technicians, employed and middle management (11.9%).

At the same time, the analysis of the social class dimension highlights Podemos as the preferred political option among the new middle classes (16.1%) and as the second chosen within the high/upper-middle class (11.0%) after the conservative Partido Popular.

On the other hand, both skilled and unskilled workers find particularly attractive the socialist option (35.6% and 26.8% respectively), while the conservative Partido Popular count on the main source of voters in the old middle classes (35.5%), those not specified (32.4%) and high/upper-middle class (182%).

Finally, Podemos' voters are mainly featured by those placed in the left-wing ideological self-location, together with those aged from 18 to 34, widening to 44 years old in the age groups, and having achieved vocational training (16.1%), higher education (14.0%), or secondary school in the second stage (13.9%).

Citizens aged 55 or older maintain their compromise with the two main parties, while the gender variable does not lead to relevant conclusions, except for the slightly higher presence of women among PSOE socialist voters.

In sum, contrary to what might be initially thought, according to post-electoral surveys on the elections to the European Parliament Podemos' voters profile is summarily defined by well-educated people, with an age range that goes from 18 to 45 years old, left-wing ideology oriented, but also people with high purchasing power.

On the other side, those with no education mostly voted for the Socialist Party (22.4%), while the ones with only primary education opted for the conservative Partido Popular (20.2%).[32]

In brief, this information highlights: (1) that Podemos gathers a wider than expected diversity of voters; (2) that many of those most affected by "the system" and the austerity measures keep supporting the "Establishment" or the current state of politics and institutional structure. See Figures 14 to 19.

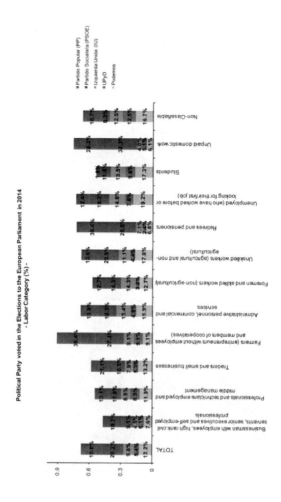

FIGURE 14

Source: Centro de Investigaciones Sociológicas (CIS) – own processing

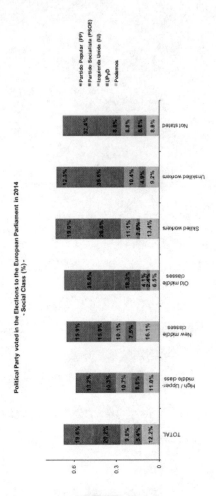

FIGURE 15

Source: Centro de Investigaciones Sociológicas (CIS) – own
processing

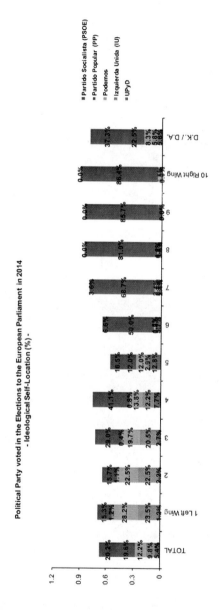

FIGURE 16

Source: Centro de Investigaciones Sociológicas (CIS) – own
processing

Los Indignados: Tides of Social Insertion in Spain

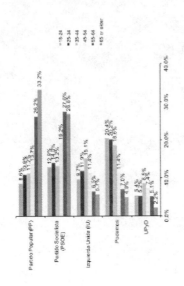

FIGURE 17
Source: Centro de
Investigaciones Sociológicas
(CIS) – own processing

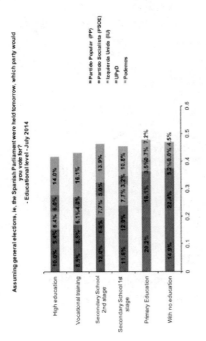

FIGURE 18
Source: Centro de
Investigaciones Sociológicas
(CIS) – own processing

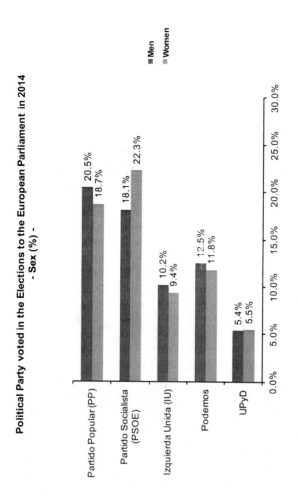

FIGURE 19

Source: Centro de Investigaciones Sociológicas (CIS) – own processing

12

The Local Elections in May 2015

Podemos' openness to the fast-breaking sociopolitical changes taking place in Spain was particularly tested in the period leading to the local elections in 2015. Podemos' decision to run for the May local and December national elections was taken in its "foundational assembly" at Vistalegre in October 2014. The new party anticipated that they already had the necessary infrastructure, counting on 800 "circles"/assemblies spread out over the country. What was to be tested was the coherence and consistency of Podemos' organizational and normative principles, the continuity in the undertaken people's empowerment process, and its rapport with other left-wing parties.

The Citizens' Congress at the Palacio Vistalegre: Podemos' internal consultation and decision-making processes for the local elections and its influence on the political arena

Between 15 September and 15 November 2014 Podemos conducts a Citizens' Congress at the Palacio Vistalegre Arena in Madrid and online using information/communication technologies (ICTs). The Congress brings together representatives in person and online from grassroots assemblies (the "circles") that had blossomed since the 2008 financial crisis and the 15 May 2011 occupations.

To be tested are the new party's organizational and normative principles, and the continuity in the process already undertaken toward people's empowerment. A contest emerges.

The contest is between two contending platforms:

- *Sumando Podemos* (Summing Up We Can), led by recently

elected Members of the European Parliament Teresa Rodríguez, Pablo Echenique, and Lola Sánchez, argue for a collective leadership of three general secretaries, and a Citizens' Council elected with a percentage of seats based on a form of random lottery. Further, they seek to guard against the oligarchic tendencies and power trips internal to party organization that Robert Michels warned against just over a century ago.

- On the other pole is *Claro Que Podemos* (CQP – Of Course We Can) led by Pablo Iglesias, Iñigo Errejón, Juan Carlos Monedero, and Carolina Bescansa. CQP argues for a single general secretary with a supporting team elected "as a whole," along with a Citizens' Council composed of 87 members. Of these 87, 17 would be the leaders of the autonomous communities' platforms and regional leaderships, with the rest to be elected by an open list system only corrected to accomplish gender quotas. The Citizens' Council would address issues of primaries or electoral coalitions with an external political force, which would subsequently need to be ratified by the "circles." Finally, there is proposed a Coordination Council composed of 10 to 15 people proposed by the General Secretary of the Party, whose policies are ratified by the Citizens' Council and not the circles "as a whole."

- Claro Que Podemos wins with 80.9%, compared to Sumando Podemos with 12.3%.

- Iglesias is elected General Secretary amidst criticism for his "vertical" (traditional hierarchical) approach rather than the Indignados movement stress on horizontal democracy. There are also mumblings that Podemos is moving toward an "electoral war machine" model.

Podemos' new leadership in consultation with the 800 "circles" decides to stand directly in the May 2015 regional elections and to support, in cities or municipalities, local grassroots candidates from the emerging new *Popular Unity* platforms, such as *Ahora Madrid* (Now Madrid), *Barcelona en Comú* (Barcelona in Common), and Atlantic Tides in Galicia. The Popular Unity candidates are to be branded with "Claro Que Podemos" approval.

The party leadership delegates the development of a draft economic program to the economists Vicenç Navarro and Juan Torres López along with the leader of the refounded communist party Izquierda Unida (IU), Alberto Garzón. The program turns out to be a Left Keynesian tract on underconsumption theory, debt restructuring, and meshing social justice with economic efficiencies.

Podemos calls for a March of Change on 31 January 2015, trying to capitalize on momentum from its November polls as Spain's leading party at 28%. Some criticize the march as a distasteful exercise of populist *personalismos* more than an expansion of grassroots politics "from below." Charges of cult of personality grow. Pressure is growing on Podemos to sustain a hybrid party model in tandem with a popular social movement, and not to appeal to some common denominator.

As we move toward the spring 2015 elections, Podemos' polls start to sag, nearing trend falls toward 18%. After its meteoric rise, Podemos loses steam as "The Alternative." Rumblings grow about the need for a more "social" than political focus. Beyond either electoral victories or manifestations of protest, there is more and more talk of transformation of the social order, an end to the era of the post-Franco Transition, a movement toward a Third Republic, toward a new concept of *the social*: a concept of the social beyond the functional model of organic solidarity developed by Emile Durkheim and used by socialist and communist parties in the twentieth century.

By April, the media are celebrating the surging Podemos of the Right, the Ciudadanos Party in Catalonia – its profile is anti-Catalan independence, free market/libertarian liberalism with an anti-union and anti-immigrant edge – led by Alberto Rivera. *Ciudadanos* (the Citizens Party) has gone nationwide with business support worried about the weakening of Prime Minister Rajoy's ruling Popular Party. Rivera even appears nude on television spots in his emphasis on the need for transparency. April polls claim Ciudadanos at 15%, but in the municipal and regional elections of 24 May, that party polls 6%.

The local elections in 2015: the arrival of the "change" and novel political coalitions and strategies

The municipal and regional elections held on 24 May 2015 resulted in left-wing coalitions controlling the 27 most important Spanish municipalities – among them, the three largest cities Madrid, Barcelona, and Valencia – comprising 10.6 million inhabitants.

The polls confirm the increasing social discontent and citizens' craving and will for change. There is a deepening social distrust toward the government and in a wider sense the political system and parties. With the strong eruption of Podemos in the Spanish political arena and with the prospect of a thoroughly new political setting, the local elections represented a good prelude to the 20 December general elections.

The conservatives' novel electoral strategies to remain in power

The Rajoy Government faced the dilemma of how to preserve its power and structural reforms in the long run, as unpopular policies and measures undermined its social support due to poor results in improving the population's living conditions. Social inequalities continued to widen. During the pre-electoral periods, traditional parties – most unabashedly and notoriously the conservatives in power – had drawn upon novel and polemic political strategies with little precedents in the Spanish democracy.

Among the most remarkable were: (1) what was termed as a "democratic regeneration," an initiative to change electoral laws for local elections: where candidates achieving 40% of votes could become the city or town mayors, preventing minority parties from doing pacts to govern; (2) the *ley mordaza* (gag law); and (3) what can be labeled as "social washing." Additionally, there were initiatives framed with the prospect of the 20-D general elections on the horizon: (4) the internationalizing of the context and consequences of the political campaign; and (5) the PP conservatives maneuvering for a possible pact with the PSOE socialists in an attempt to assure control over the national government and institutions – or with others such as the new center-right party Ciudadanos.

The most paradoxical of strategies are those devised with an eye toward the electoral results regarding secessionisms – here, the ones historically present in Catalonia and the Basque Country. These seek to gain control of hundreds or thousands of local institutions. These are left-wing and social democratic separatist alternatives with increasing social support, displacing the conservative secessionism traditionally more influential in the sociopolitical arena due to the current socio-economic and institutional crisis. What re-emerges on the Right is propaganda about threats to the so-called "unity of the Spanish nation," as opposed to the theme of a building a Plurinational Spain, or a United Kingdom of the Spanish Peoples.

First, the "democratic regeneration" finally was not to be carried out by the PP for the local elections in 2015. What was afoot was the strategy of alliances decided by parties, and not voters, once the electoral period was over. The plan triggers numerous suspicions, as it reveals the Rajoy Government's strategy to keep or increase its governing capacity by whatever means possible over the territory, and its intention to hamper other alternatives to govern.

Second, the government's approval of the Public Safety

Act – also known as *ley mordaza* (gag law) – triggered intense demonstrations in the streets (December 2014) and complaints from organizations such as the United Nations Human Rights Committee and the European Court of Human Rights. This Public Safety Act limits the fundamental rights of citizens' demonstration or freedom of speech with sanctions without juridical mediation: for example, a penalty of 600 to 30,000 euros for trying to prevent an eviction, not identifying oneself to a police officer, disobeying a police officer, or broadcasting images taken from demonstrations. It also affects immigrants and their probable expulsion from the country ("hot returns"), obstructing and pulling the plug on their right to asylum. For many, the gag law resembles the Franco dictatorship's Public Order Act of 1959.

Third, the *social washing* mentioned earlier in this book parallels the practice of "green washing," i.e. marketing campaigns from the most polluting companies to show an environmentalist image. Social washing denotes the attempt of traditional parties to align themselves rhetorically with citizens' growing concern toward "the social" by exhibiting a false image of being "socially concerned," while all the while unpopular austerity measures are implemented. For example, through the sudden announcement of measures targeting the improvement of labor conditions for civil servants, or reiterating the state's support to the unemployed or others. It is all a superficial image of showing social concern, in contrast to making any real depth structure changes.

Fourth, the internationalization of the political campaign aims to explicitly show citizens the support from other European political leaders – e.g. the European conservatives David Cameron or Angela Merkel – for the current government and the ongoing austerity reforms, or against secessionism in Catalonia.

Fifth, and never before witnessed in the recent Spanish democratic period, PP conservatives plot for a possible pact with the socialists (traditional political opponents) or the emergent center-right party Ciudadanos, targeting a "joint front" to counterbalance the emergent left-wing parties or coalitions which they form. This is expressed as citizen duty to build a national unity government as a "matter of State" in pre-electoral communications.

More *social washing* as response: Podemos and its influence in other parties' internal organization and communication patterns

In many ways, Podemos' influence in the political arena can equally be noticed by other parties emulating some of the new party's novel ways of self-organization and approaches to citizen-based horizontality, public debates, and consensus. For example, for the first time all affiliates from the socialist Partido Socialista and the communist Izquierda Unida vote for their respective Secretary-General (or main leader). And at the local level some leaders from the conservative Partido Popular do explicitly agree with this possibility. The socialists' new leader Pedro Sánchez starts open assemblies in different towns and cities to discuss and gather ideas from citizens to set his electoral program, gives priority to the recruitment of new affiliates or social leaders to head local candidatures, and breaks with the communication strategy patterns in his party, participating in primetime entertainment TV programs (something unusual among Spanish politicians).

The new Indignados mayors: *Barcelona en Comú* (Barcelona in Common) and *Ahora Madrid* (Madrid Right Now) – the response but not necessarily the answer

Come Saturday 13 June, Popular Unity mayors are installed in Madrid (Manuela Carmena), Barcelona (Ada Colau), Zaragoza (Pedro Santisteve), A Coruña (Xulio Ferreiro), Santiago de

Compostela (Martiño Noriega), Cádiz (José María González), Badalona (Dolors Sabater), and Pamplona (Joseba Asiron). In addition, Valencia is governed by a coalition of Compromís, Podemos, and PSOE, with a PSOE provincial president, Ximo Puig, and Compromís mayor Joan Ribó. See Picture 3.

PICTURE 3
Newly elected mayors in the May 2015 elections – May 2015
Courtesy: Ahora Madrid

After years of warily looking upward at the verticality of institutions, thousands of people throng the streets near their town halls to celebrate, woken up from the "social washing" cant of the widely discredited elite. Neither the Ahora Madrid elected mayor in Madrid, Manuela Carmena, nor the elected mayor of Barcelona, Ada Colau (Guanyem Barcelona/Barcelona en Comú), is dependent on Podemos. Each comes to power in a coalition with PSOE. An emerging popular majority is no longer resigned, and is increasingly referred to as "Popular Unity" governments.

There is a merging into a single political force crystallized in the initiative *Ganemos* (Let's Win) and *Barcelona en Común* (Barcelona in Common). This is a project led by Ada Colau, the head of Guanyem Barcelona and the guiding activist in the social campaign against evictions. Colau announces she is endeavoring to coordinate a "great political majority": arguing this as a historic responsibility where all the forces in the field are "condemned to understand each other." See Pictures 4 and 5.

PICTURE 4

**Plaça Catalunya – Colau's Barcelona en Común speech for the May
2015 general election results – May 2015
Courtesy: Barcelona en Común**

With the claim "the right to decide everything," the success of these initiatives highly depends on the collective capacity to conciliate (without voiding) the diversity of ideological and

PICTURE 5
Manuela Carmena's celebration of the May 2015 local elections
results. Courtesy: Ahora Madrid

political sensibilities. This amounts to the ways and means of understanding sociopolitical life and identities within a common project and horizon. As such, this is a shift from the ideological fragmentation and contestation to the function of leadership in governance.

13

The 20-D General Election and Its Wake: Moving into 2016

The new political forces of Podemos and Popular Unity Confluences confront the challenge of meeting the high social expectations and hope created. There is recognition of the need for operational and electoral structures. But this will not be free of frictions, given the horizontality principle intrinsic to assemblies. Podemos and the other civic platforms count on the fluent complementarity of horizontal and vertical communication and coordination between the "circles," assemblies, and the elected and pacted governance group.

A pragmatic policy of "pacting" emerges. There is an implicit tendency toward what is now tactically called *Confluence* with a capital letter C. This is an emphasis on Popular Unity beyond Podemos in order to unite a social majority. The Popular Party attacks PSOE leader Pedro Sánchez for making "deals" with Popular Unity candidates at the local level, as a *popular front strategy* emerges for the general election on 20 December 2015. Despite his earlier protestations that he never "pacts" or would work with Podemos, Sánchez winds up supporting the Popular Unity pacting strategy of Confluence. On 16 June, the newspaper *El Periódico* proclaims, "Sánchez Justifies Pacts with Iglesias: Do Not Call Us a Caste Anymore." IU leader Garzón writes an op-ed piece titled "Popular Unity Is the Only Way." PSOE knows public opinion is flowing leftward toward Popular Unity Confluence.

Juan Carlos Monedero had resigned from the Podemos leadership by 31 March 2015 in a conflict with the so-called verticalist *Errejónistas* within Podemos: claiming they were straying from the 15-M spirit of Indignados, and taking on a more traditional social democratic economic policy mold. He argued for the need to maintain "social" forms, to emphasize building a "social bloc" and resisting thinking like a traditional party. Monedero hinted that Errejón's faction tended to want to meet to decide how social pacts would emerge, rather than recognize the importance of their spontaneity and dialogue with the party instrument. Monedero was soon featured with former Cordoba mayor Julio Anguita, a founder of IU, as well as Alberto Garzón, promoting a "popular front" strategy.

Confluence platforms resist any replay of top-down politics, "verticalism" as it is called in Spain. "Confluence" is the term that characterizes a new political culture of *social pacting*. The new mayors are referred to increasingly as Indignados mayors. There is a revival of flying the purple flag of 15-M as a symbol of the Confluence of different forms of "Popular Unity." The day after the 25 May elections, Iglesias reads the tea leaves, and acknowledges the emergence of Confluence, a popular front strategy of at least five parties, even with alliances with PSOE. He talks of Podemos not being a "general" party, "but one that is open to the participation and role of all instruments committed to change...We need to weave bridges between all sectarianism." He argues this after having argued provocatively – in an essay that appears in the May–June 2015 issue (#93) of the *New Left Review* – that PSOE "will either accept the leadership of Podemos or commit suicide by subordination to the Popular Party." It is increasingly apparent that PSOE pacting with Ciudadanos – as in the installation of PSOE Andalucía leader Susana Díaz – has increasingly dangerous overtones for Sánchez.

After all the spinning of theory in the Podemos leadership over Ernesto Laclau's Left populism, the so-called "empty signifier" that Laclau mystically invoked now takes on meaning: "Anyone except the Popular Party. Let's win the general election." Popular Unity Confluence is widely recognized as the very next stage, pragmatically beyond the stage of tensions between political party opportunists and ideological purists.

In the end, neither a victory for party or ideology, but a victory for social movement. Podemos has accomplished a large electoral advance for the Left as a whole, and continues as the epicenter of a Popular Unity Confluence movement grounded in the spirit and commitments of the Indignados of 15-M.

Toward the 20 December general elections: Ahora en Común and the rebellion of the new Indignados mayors contra Podemos

After the May 2015 elections, the civic Tides and the Popular Unity Platforms claim their leadership for the "change" previously centered on Podemos. Once the institutional control of the main Spanish cities and towns has been achieved, the new "Indignados mayors" proclaim their autonomy and argue for the highly popular principle of Confluence of different left-wing parties and local grassroots initiatives fighting for social rights. Beyond the proved efficiency of this electoral "formula," the aim is to reconnect with the origins and essence of the Indignados protests back in 2011.

Podemos faced a dilemma:

(1) of whether to keep faithful to its initial ideals based on a totally new way of understanding politics and citizens' approach and interaction to politics; or

(2) of whether to tilt into a "softer" position to widen its base as a "critical mass" of potential voters (especially, the middle classes) while avoiding intruders in the leadership's democratic centralist policy-making processes.

As the timeline above in Chapter 2 shows, Podemos displays a tendency toward "a *personalismo*" of Pablo Iglesias as The Leader, and a discourse shift to social democracy. More and more moderate language and arguments seem to characterize this new party and make it resemble more a traditional party instead of serving as a "real" alternative.

The "rebellion" of the Indignados mayors showed a concern for not missing the "historic opportunity" for consolidating and sustaining the insertion and the embeddedness of the new sense of "the social" in a reciprocal solidarity that comes with the new resilient social pacting.

The Indignados movement comes to focus on issues of Confluence coalitions

After the local elections in May 2015, the investiture of the "new mayors" in most important Spanish cities symbolizes the strength and possibilities of the Indignados' legacy and its long-run influence in the Spanish sociopolitical arena – especially the Confluence of social forces questioning the legitimacy of a discredited Transition State. Their focus is framed as a proposed Confluence of movement actors for an alternative government regime. An alternative with *staying power* – having electoral and institutionalizing force, rather than a spontaneous and passing phenomenon. This is first manifested during the electoral contest to the Catalan Parliament on 27 September.

The new scenario of political fragmentation also inaugurates a new era of know-how on social pacting – not just in solidarity-based community networks of exchanges, but also in the conformation of local and national governments and political coalitions.

The Confluence process will be driven by sociopolitical actors such as Podemos, IU, the "new mayors" elected in May, and other left-wing and ecology parties at the national level, as well as the local alternatives of Ada Colau in Barcelona, the Tides in Galicia, and the Pact to theValencians with Compromís. See Picture 6.

PICTURE 6
The political leaders Ada Colau and Pablo Iglesias – December 2015
Courtesy: Podemos

On 15 June Podemos starts a four-month participatory process to develop its political program for the 20 December general elections for the Spanish Parliament. Particularly, the electoral and confluence strategy adopted between 15 and 22 July represents a shift from initial positions when Podemos limited pre-electoral agreements only to the "historic" communities (Catalonia, Galicia, the Basque Country, Valencia, and Baleares). With about 12% of participation rate (45,000 out of 375,000 of those registered) and the support of 85% of participants, a Confluence platform document was framed by two main guidelines:

(1) The *confluence or alliances with other sociopolitical forces* would take place just at the local level (the province), thus avoiding either electoral pacts at the national level or an explicit post-electoral support for other political

forces; and

(2) The Podemos logo and trademark would appear prominently in the listing of such provincial confluence on the electoral ballot.

In so doing, Podemos is the first Spanish political party submitting to consultation its strategy of pre-electoral alliances. This participatory process would trigger a debate on how the consultation question was posed. The participatory values in this process were thrashed out: "What were affiliates to be asked?" The result would read as follows.

Do you agree that Podemos' Citizens' Council, in order to move forward in development of a popular and citizen candidacy, sets agreements with various political actors and civil society given that:

(1) agreements are established at a territorial scale (never more than autonomic level, (2) [we] always keep Podemos' logo and name in the first place on the ballot even if that means attending the general elections in some territories with alliance formulas [Podemos – X]

The "new mayors" would explicitly claim their own identity and autonomy – differentiated from Podemos. Further, they rejected their "electoral use" by Podemos, claiming that the local confluences led the "alternative" sociopolitical agenda. One of their main arguments is that the electoral victories achieved in the local elections were due to the Confluence social pacting between different political forces and social movements. Such pacts were an inclusive and autonomous, rather than a party-based, process of convergence.

This point of view is supported on 5 September when the *Ciudades por el Bien Común* (Cities for the Common Good) lay the foundation for the creation of a network of municipalities.

The general goal is the better organization and coordination of the municipalities for "the change." Signing on are mayors from Madrid, Zaragoza, Barcelona, Badalona, A Coruña, Santiago de Compostela, Iruña, and Cádiz. The goal is not just to discuss experiences of local government, but the coordination of social pacting initiatives and the strengthening of public participation and accountability.

Confluence sentiment articulated in the platform Ahora en Común (AeC)

On 12 September a new Confluence platform, Ahora en Común (AeC), holds its first general assembly and proceeds to define the framework for the left-wing forces' unity in the 20-D general elections – as a Popular Unity candidature or *Confluence*. Significantly, as a *tide away* from the Socialist Workers Party.

The platform framework is initiated by Izquierda Unida and the ecologists of the Equo Party. It comprises over 1000 affiliates; and sets its ethical and programmatic premises, aiming to resemble the process followed by Ahora Madrid, Barcelona en Comú, or Zaragoza en Común in the past May 2015 local elections. The AeC Confluence platform document:

(1) claims a "viral" origin;
(2) challenges Iglesias' plan for the general elections; and
(3) appeals to 15-M to launch its Confluence project.

Ahora en Común (AeC) had been launched in early July 2015 with a manifesto – signed by 30,000 people according to its promoters – on behalf of this greater sense of Confluence. At the same time, the *Encontro Cidadán por unha Marea Galega* (Citizens' Gathering for a Galician Tide) is organized in the city of Santiago de Compostela – in the region of Galicia – and the autonomous parliamentary group *Na Marea* (In Tide) is created. This platform is constituted by both nationalists and non-nationalist parties:

BNG, Podemos, the secessionist political forces Compromiso por Galicia y Cerna, Esquerda Unida (EU), and Equo y Espazo Ecosocialista. AeC is envisioned as a greater Confluence featured by parties from the leftist ideological spectrum ranging from social democracy to communism, through eco-socialism and international socialism.

However, shortly after its launch – also in September – the initial promoters of Ahora en Común quit the platform, arguing that Izquierda Unida (IU) is becoming its "main reference." The platform is criticized for its "politicization." What prevails, they argue, is not the "citizens' assemblies" but a rebooted *Realpolitik* of reformist political apparatuses.

Likewise, Podemos argues that Ahora en Común is not the adequate space for the Popular Unity's Confluence and considers IU as part of *La Casta* – that is, as a party from the establishment as the inheritor of Santiago Carrillo's Spanish Communist Party (PSE). Podemos argues for getting beyond the left- and right-wing ideological axis logic as a clear contrast. Many of IU's members are reluctant to accept the union with Podemos.

Two weeks later the 27 September (27-S) elections to the Catalan Parliament will represent a milestone in the Confluence process. Political strategies and discussions that had ensued so far would then be substantially changed. Podemos' electoral failures in the Catalonia provincial elections on 27 September (27-S) lead it to argue that the social discourse regarding the right to an autonomous Catalonia is dominated by the right-wing discourse of Artur Mas's Popular Unity Candidacy party.

Podemos itself is criticized for its deficient consideration of secessionist sentiments. The dismissal of its regional general secretary would lead to a shift in the negotiation process with other political forces and social movements focused on the coming 20 December (20-D) general elections campaign.

Two days later Pablo Echenique – EDP Podemos' leader in the region of Aragon – will reach an agreement with Ahora

Aragón en Común for a joint candidature for the next general elections. Negotiations between both organizations will last until 10 October after Alberto Garzón and Pablo Iglesias break off conversations for 20-D general elections joint candidates. The Zaragoza en Común Confluence was one of the few experiences of a coalition in which Podemos shared an electoral list with IU in the May 2015 municipal elections for "political change."

Ahora en Común fails to gather in Madrid the left-wing parties wanting to pact for a single-list with Podemos for the 20-D general elections. This motivates the launching of *Unidad Popular en Común* (Popular Unity in Common) on 2 October. This is a new left-wing Confluence platform placed outside of the PSOE. It gathers the main representatives from a wide range of Indignados groups:

> Ahora Madrid leaders Pablo Soto and Pablo Carmona; the Fundación de los Comunes and *Traficantes de Sueños* (Traffickers of Dreams) associated with Emmanuel Rodríguez; Ahora en Común; part of Federal IU; Convocatoria por Madrid (led by former IU leader Tania Sánchez); Equo; *Decide en Común* (Decide in Common, led by the former socialist member Alberto Sotillos); *Somos Izquierda* (We Are Left-Wing, founded by the former socialist leader Beatriz Talegón); the party *Por un Mundo Más Justo* (For a Fairer World); *Por La Izquierda* (To the Left), headed by former judge Baltasar Garzón with its platform *Convocatoria Cívica* (Civic Call); Izquierda Abierta (led by IU's deputy Gaspar Llamazares); *Recortes Cero-Los Verdes* (The Greens' "Zero-Cuts"); and Cristina Almeida (former communist and IU's militant and historic labor lawyer).

A few days later, Podemos proclaims a definitive "No" to any strategy of joint candidates with Alberto Garzón and the IU in the 20-D general election. On the contrary, Podemos party leaders invite IU's leader to become part of Podemos' list. Podemos is motivated by their apparent drop in the public opinion polls. So now Podemos seeks to invite to their political project socially recognized individuals from the Left and the intellectual world. A debate ensues on the possible consequences of this schism between IU and Podemos. On the one hand, it is argued that this division could result in a significant impact on the political landscape with the addition of the 50 deputies that could be achieved. This is projected to come from the addition of medium-sized *circumscriptions* – i.e. bounded political constituencies. These have been traditionally monopolized by PP/PSOE bipartisanship – instead of the 36 targeted by Podemos for itself.

The electoral system penalizes minor parties; and Podemos argues that "the sum of acronyms" does not automatically bring the sum of the votes. Podemos leaders emphasize that IU's marked leftist ideology frightens the population's moderate sectors. Specifically, Podemos initiated a strategic shift once it became a popular party trying, with its "floating empty signifier" tact, not to be linked either to anti-capitalism parties or to social democracy.

In that sense, Podemos is concerned that a relevant portion of its voters do not come from the classical left-wing ideological constellation. On the contrary, the economic crisis, the eruption of multiple corruption cases, and the widening of socio-economic inequalities entails transversal/criss-crossing flows: first, among the traditional socialist electorate, but particularly among people who would never vote for IU.

Sustained in their revised floating signifier tact of "different political eco-systems," Podemos' position at the national level does not impede Podemos and IU in concurring together: for example, on a regional/local level in Catalonia and Galicia, or in seeking partners in other territories. The joint ventures between both parties can be observed just in localities or regions – where they had already been a political force occupying particular political space. Catalonia, Galicia, and Valencia had become the May 2015 local elections' great achievements where Confluence coalitions built on conditions that had already existed.

The Confluence process with Podemos in articulating platforms is further interrupted when on 8 October Decide en Común (the party led by the former PSOE politician Alberto Sotillos) breaks with Podemos. This occurs even though 65% of this organization's "members and supporters" voted to "work toward a Confluence with Podemos" – and against the option of seeking the unity of the Left "in any of the possible lists as Ahora en Común." Their rationale, Decide en Común argues, is that Podemos had not shown authentic willingness for a "real" Confluence, only electoral scheming.

Nonetheless, on that same day, the Confluence process is pushed ahead further with the news from Catalonia. Barcelona en Comú and its main leader, Ada Colau, decide to concur in the 20-D general elections campaign under the candidature brand *En Comú Podem* (In Common We Can). This candidature strategy aims to have its own parliamentary group in the Congress headed by the noted Catalonia history university professor Xavier Domènech – who is also leader of the academic/political movement to repeal the Law of Forgetting and restore the memory of the Civil War of the 1930s. The candidature brand also includes other leftist forces such as Podem, Iniciativa per Catalunya Verds (ICV), Esquerra Unida (EUiA), and Barcelona en Comú.

Among its several challenges, En Común Podem seeks to achieve a self-determination referendum for Catalonia. This new coalition expects to totally change the poor results Podemos obtained in the September electoral campaign; to pose different senses of "autonomy of Catalonia"; and to become the winning political alternative in Catalonia. Critical here is Ada Colau's strength, which lies in her legitimacy from her activism leading the Anti-Evictions Platform (PAH) from the time of the outbreak of the Crisis.

Podemos refuses, however, to create joint candidatures for the 20-D general election with *Ahora en Común* (AeC – Now in Common). And Alberto Garzón (IU) emerges to lead AeC – replacing former IU leader Cayo Lara. Garzón leads this platform in holding primary elections during the following days (22–26 October). Garzón's candidate list is called *Ahora con Alberto Garzón* (Now with Alberto Garzón). Among its top ten in the electoral list are popular leaders from the social, feminist, and ecologies movements, former socialists, and Izquierda Abierta candidates. The latter are led by Gaspar Llamazares, along with some members of the former IU in the Community of Madrid expelled by the federal IU organization *Convergencia de la Izquierda* (the Left Convergence). On 27 October Alberto Garzón's list overwhelmingly wins the Ahora en Común primaries, achieving the top five places in the candidature list for the 20-D general elections. Garzón will next vainly try to negotiate with Podemos for a joint bid.[30]

Next, on 28 October, 55% of the ecologist party Equo's affiliates accept a pact with Podemos for the 20-D general elections. Its main leader, Juantxo Lopez de Uralde, will head the electoral list in Álava, thus definitely quitting from the Confluence project of *Unidad Popular en Común* (the new brand for AeC).

Two weeks later (7 November), Alberto Sotillos of *Decide en Común* (Decide in Common) – one of the major signings for Alberto Garzón's list for Madrid – quits Unidad Popular; along with the coalition calling itself *Por un Mundo Más Justo* (For a Fairer World); and *Por La Izquierda* (To the Left). Por La Izquierda is the platform promoted by former activist and investigating magistrate Baltasar Garzón. (This is the same magistrate who in 1998 had an international warrant issued for the arrest of former Chilean Augusto Pinochet for the deaths and torture of Spanish citizens.)

Two days later on 31 October, Podemos submits its 20-D

elections draft political program and names to its electoral lists: that is, Podemos submits its lists to its more than 300,000 affiliates. In the general elections voting process, measures could be voted individually or as complete programs – the latter as a variant known as *listas plancha* (griddle lists), full programs that include about 400 or 500 measures.

Likewise, Podemos creates a set of filters for the acceptance of proposals. This allows Podemos to exclude from the program some of the most radical proposals while seeking some balance between those committed to "participatory democracy" and those having more strategic objectives. Here Iglesias emphasizes "common sense, transversal, and transformative measures." The party expects to collect between 800 and 1000 platform proposals from 10,000 experts, civil organizations, regional party leaders, heads of the sectoral areas, and individuals.

The result is that Podemos sets the "right to decide" for Catalonia (and other nationalities of the state) as one of the five pillars of its 20-D political program and campaign. The other four pillars are:

- the changing of the electoral system (towards its proportionality);
- the fight against corruption and the "revolving doors" in politics;
- the autonomy of the judicial power; and
- total guarantees on labor rights, health, education, or housing.

This is in contrast to the period when the Podemos Party's participation schemes were much more assembly-oriented and linked to the restructuring of the debt default or the minimum universal income or retirement at 60 years old.

Politically, this consultation process represents a strategic moderation of some of Podemos' main tenets and identity as it aims to increase its options for governing the country. Some examples are past demands for the opening of a constitutional process; in continuously attacking the so-called *La Casta*; and emphasizing the state's sovereign debt and the national financial sector's audit and restructuring instead of default or nationalization. Generally, the party's emphasis changes to reforming the tax system; pursuing a modification of the production model; seeking to reverse the social welfare cuts; and probing the workings of de-politicization in public administration. A result of this consultation process is that 96% – in 50 out of 52 electoral constituencies – of the headliners for the 20-D general elections are Pablo Iglesias' trusted compatriots.

About six weeks before the 20-D general elections (7 November), left-wing organizations reach agreements for the Confluence in Catalonia, Valencia, and Galicia. In Catalonia the Confluence is represented by *En Comú Podem* (In Common We Can), in Valencia by the joint candidature between Compromís and Podemos; and in the Basque Country and Navarra the left-wing nationalists (EH Bildu, which in the last elections has been called Amaiur). Particularly in Navarra, the novelty is the coalition for the Senate between Bildu, Geroa Bai, Podemos, and Izquierda-Ezkerra.

Nonetheless, these Confluence agreements stand only for the electoral concurrence for this one time for seats in the Congress. The Tides of Social Insertion intend to form their own parliamentary group once they reach the Congress of Deputies. In the rest of the country, Podemos concurs with the platforms of its competitors, Izquierda Unida with the *Unidad Popular* (Popular Unity) platform.

Particularly, Podemos agrees to support a referendum in Catalonia in accord with Ada Colau's political project En Comú Podem. Podemos leaders invoke the pledge to a "Plurinational Spain," to "a nation of the Spanish peoples," made at its October 2014 founding Congress at Vistalegre. Ada Colau had decided not to join the Catalunya Sí que es Pot political campaign for the regional elections on 27-S. But for the 20-D general elections, Colau and the vice president of Valencia, Compromís' Mònica Oltra, become key reference group opinion leaders. The confirming effect of Ada Colau's and Oltra's endorsements increases Podemos' options in Catalonia and Valencia (see Picture 7). En Comú Podem candidates are now expected to totally change the results obtained in the 27-S election. Nonetheless, the defense of the referendum with Iglesias and Errejón – the right to decide – risks losing votes in the rest of Spain.

PICTURE 7
Mónica Oltra in a political meeting of Compromís in May 2011
From Wikimedia Commons/Ingolll
Courtesy: Compromís

Note, here, the kind of "double discourse" resorted to: to vote in the general elections alongside Podemos, so that the aspiration to form their own group in the Congress of Deputies can give wings to En Comú Podem. To reiterate, the stability of the Confluence/Popular Unity is based on the autonomy of the different territorial sociopolitical forces and their identities – En Marea, En Comú Podem, and Compromís/Podemos/És el Moment).

The 20-D elections – some conclusions

- Podemos achieves 20% more votes than PSOE in cities with over 100,000 inhabitants.

Podemos and Ciudadanos are sustained mostly by the urban vote (47.3% and 46.4% respectively). Both formations got almost one out of two votes in cities with over 100,000 inhabitants. The urban portion of the total vote of the Popular Party (PP) is lower (42.9%); whereas the PSOE's urban support percentage drops to 36.9%.

The Socialists have managed to beat Podemos in 23 of the 55 cities with over 100,000 inhabitants – ten of them located in Andalucia, its traditional granary of votes. The PSOE defeats Podemos only in two of the ten largest (Seville and Malaga), and underperforms in the rest: Madrid, Barcelona, Valencia, Zaragoza, Las Palmas, Murcia, Bilbao, and Palma de Mallorca. The Socialists secure the most urban votes on the whole in Spain – 5,530,779 vs. 5,189,463 – but in absolute terms, Podemos attracted more votes in large cities than the PSOE, specifically 414,388 (representing a 20% differential).

- The PP won the plurality in most large cities and in 32 of the 55 most populated cities, even exceeding the percentage of votes that they got on the national level (28.7%).

Podemos and its allies start the new year of 2016 as the third political force in the Congress with 69 deputies. In spite of the good results, this party did not yet surpass the Socialists. The debate extends to the possible Confluence between IU and

Podemos that would have obtained 13 more seats and the Left could win more seats from the Right in terms of 19 deputies.

These results and possibilities are structured by the complexity of the Spanish electoral system that is governed by the D'Hondt rules, with a threshold minimum of 3% to enter the Congress of Deputies' distribution of proportional representation seats. The number of seats resulting from more Podemos-aligned Confluence strategies could have increased by 13, reaching a total of 84 (compared to 69 for Podemos and two for Popular Unity (UP) obtained on 20-D), considering the amount of votes that went to UP in each of the districts.

- In breaking the predominant PP-PSOE bipartisan party hegemony over the Transition State, the electorate now will question: Whether there is a willingness of the four major parties system – along with Popular Unity and Nationalist smaller parties – to work together in the pursuit of common goals; and to sustain a belief of all the peoples in Spain to govern themselves in an epoch of increasing vulnerability.

Despite the leap forward from the Franquist Era, there is a patchy social safety net with chronic inefficiency in both the delivery of and access to public welfare services. The path to democracy has been more of a path to economic liberalization with heavy costs not equally shared. That path is marked by a continued social stratification with a heavy accent on the power of the older connected families of the Franco/Bourbon eras.

- Iñigo Errejón announces the program that Podemos will pursue:

(1) helping people on the verge of poverty or already poor even if no longer evicted;

(2) judicial reform and effective separation of powers within a state dedicated to the realization of democracy in Spain;

(3) effective safeguards against corruption;

(4) effective financial regulation, especially of shadow banking;

(5) effectively monitored limits to the financing of political parties;

(6) reversal in cuts in social spending;

(7) reversal of trend to privatization of public services;

(8) recovery of rights against Law 25 against evictions and power outages and cutting off of gas to households;

(9) repealing of labor market reforms under Prime Ministers Rajoy and Rodríguez Zapatero;

(10) modifying of Article 135 of the Spanish Constitution that had put priority on the interests of debt collectors;

(11) restoring and further developing a sustainable safety net for social spending (referred to as a "social ground") at both the national and regional levels;

(12) expansionary economic policies to stimulate an innovation economy;

(13) commitment to renewable energy as well as energy efficiencies;

(14) modernization of the education system;

(15) further democratization of the political system;

(16) commitment to a Plurinational Spain on the basis of some sort of federal/polycentric model; and

(17) repeal of the "gag law" censoring debate in the public sphere.

- When many citizens vote for Podemos, they do not necessarily support a referendum on Catalonian autonomy.

Rather, they are supporting both (1) a counterbalancing of the political class associated with governing the Transition State; as well as (2) a general *social insertion* into a perceived incomplete and stalled tandem of civil society and the state.

- Irene Martín (2015), among others, raises the issue of how "tight" the relationship is between the Podemos and Indignados social movements.

Debates continue, noting that the Popular Unity candidates at the local levels express much better the idea of "Movement Left" akin to Evo Morales' MAS (Movement for Socialism) in Bolivia. Specifically, what is raised is the move by the Podemos General Secretary and the Citizens' Council away from emphasis on horizontal circles to verticality and pragmatism.

- The success of Confluence in the 20-D general elections strengthens Ada Colau. The alliance between Colau and Podemos becomes the first political option in Catalonia – with 12 seats (24.7% of votes achieved in the 20-D in Catalonia) – and a result not ever achieved by Artur Mas and his CUP.

The combination of the political capital of Pablo Iglesias and Colau can explain this successful alliance in the wake of the claim for the sovereignty/autonomy referendum in Catalonia. This is especially so because they have created a popular alliance strategy that did not repeat the mistakes made by Catalunya Sí que es Pot when campaigning in regional elections in September.

Some clues that do explain this successful Alliance are: (1) the claim for the sovereignty referéndum in Catalonia; and (2) the combination of the political capital of Pablo Iglesias and Ada Colau. This is especially true for the latter suggestion because neither political leader repeated the mistake made in Catalunya Sí que es Pot campaigning in the September regional elections.

- Colau and her partners announce that they are intent on leading a new party separate from Podemos (26 January 2016).

The speed and intensity of changes taking place in the Spanish sociopolitical scenario have a determinant effect on the complementary yet respective emergent political projects of Ada Colau or Podemos. Thus, the sequence of Colau's approach is first political, then institutional, and finally, focused on party organization. The general idea of Colau's project is to articulate a new political economy and with it a new sociopolitical vision. Colau aims to include Podem/Podemos in this project without exposing her own popular movement to vulnerabilities that open up in the party led by Pablo Iglesias.

The Catalonian parties discuss the initials of their respective brands: what they should be and how should appear within the new formation led by Ada Colau. The collective decision: Podemos, ICV, EUiA y Barcelona en Comú. However, these Catalonian parties have not yet settled on an organizational model. Some prefer a very tight integration, while others want to maintain the identity of each party. This involves moving from the electoral cooperation to a permanent pact. This would mean establishing a party in Catalonia which brings together Podemos, ICV, and EUiA y Barcelona en Comú (and with the exception of the CUP), which already collaborated in the municipal initiative and in Catalunya Sí que es Pot (without support from En Comú Podem). Some in Colau's movement are in favor of a very tight integration; others prefer to keep the "identity" of each party within the collaboration.

- In the negotiations to form a coalition government headed by PSOE leader Pedro Sánchez, Susana Díaz warns Sánchez that he cannot decide to pact with any other party by himself. Sánchez is accountable to the PSOE Federal

Committee composed of regional leaders. There is an obvious fissure between an old guard and a newer bloc looking to pull PSOE out of the shell Zapatero got it into in acceding to EU and IMF pressures without consultation.

Sánchez was the candidate who succeeded PSOE leader Alfredo Pérez Rubalcaba. Sánchez was not the candidate of former Prime Minister Rodríguez Zapatero, who had supported Eduardo Madina, when Pérez Rubalcaba resigned after the Podemos successful eruption at the polls for Euro MPs in May 2014. In the internecine juggling within the PSOE, Rubalcaba intercedes for Sánchez and pressures the Andalucian PSOE leader/regional president Díaz. Rubalcaba calls on Díaz to refrain from discussing PSOE, to refrain from creating a political pact with Ciudadanos, and to give Sánchez time to build a Coalition of the Left with Podemos, IU, and Popular Unity on the model of the coalition that new Prime Minister Antonio Costa has built in Portugal.

- Sánchez and the PSOE have more to lose than Iglesias and Podemos if a pact to form a Coalition of the Left Government fails, and another election needs to be called for 26 June 2016.

Podemos has more margin to take risks in holding off from immediate entry into government, so as to squeeze PSOE into concessions and to sustain the movement for a rupture from the "old politics" of the 1978 Transition State. PSOE does not seem to want to bargain on the issue of choice/referenda on autonomy issues of the nationalities. (A stubborn bloc of old PSOE politics may not understand that Catalonia may actually prefer to stay in a new Plurinational Spain.)

- Sánchez is attempting to cobble together the first multiparty government in the new democracy since 1978.

His pact with Alberto Rivera of Ciudadanos (C's) secures a U-turn from C's support of another Rajoy Government – which when C's leader Alberto Rivera supported it in January could only amount to 163 of the necessary 176 seats needed for investiture. He does so without consulting PSOE regional affiliates. Sánchez says he seeks a Government of Change. He is also playing a card that the European Union financial overlords could force Rajoy's PP to abstain at the last minute to facilitate a minority Sánchez Government that avoids the risks of having Podemos in government.

- Sánchez attempts to show leadership capability in leading Spain to the next stage in "the Transition to Democracy." At the same time, he is holding off the challenge of Susana Díaz by postponing the calling of the PSOE Congress which has to meet to decide whether to renew his leadership of PSOE.

Sánchez is exploring the Ciudadanos alliance, knowing it cannot succeed, so as to structure the negotiating game with both Podemos and PSOE regional leaders. Sánchez also understands the party constraints on any bargaining he must do with Iglesias, Errejón, Enchenique, and Irene Montero, Coordinator of the Office of the General Secretary and Deputy Spokesperson at the Congress of Deputies. Particularly, he is aware that the Socialists of Catalonia recently reorganized themselves after tossing out members with autonomy/secession sentiments. He is more comfortable with the anti-secessionist discourse for his particular federalist position.

- Iglesias is seen as tempted to serve in a PSOE-led Sánchez Government as Vice Prime Minister for Media and Intelligence matters, as long as Podemos holds a number of ministerial posts.

Such speculation provokes Podemos founder Juan Carlos Monedero who tells *El Pais:*
"Some want to enter government as soon as possible even though the circumstances are not optimal. Others meanwhile want to continue consolidating their claim to represent change, and they will not subordinate themselves so urgently to policies which are not their own."
Iglesias fires back that the Podemos leadership is not engaged in some "competition for control of bureaucracies and resources that would turn them into what [they] always fought: being just another party within the State Machine."

- After 100 days of negotiations, Sánchez is seeking "cross-government" of 199 deputies with Ciudadanos, Podemos, and IU/Popular Unity, knowing he has until 2 May, otherwise the 26 June general election is triggered.
- By the start of April, Alberto Rivera announces that he welcomes working with Podemos. Iñigo Errejón remarks that Ciudadanos is committed to some of the same issues of "democratic regneration" as Podemos: a fairer electoral system; fairer rules governing the Congress of Deputies; independence of the media; transparency.
- Errejón and Iglesias increasingly use the term "to the Valencian" (toward a Valencian anti-Popular Party coalition government) where Podemos in May and June 2015 joined with PSOE, IU, and Compromís.
- Pablo Enchenique, as the newly elected organizational secretary of Podemos, details "Operation Lace-Up": a transformative program to "move toward a less centralized organization" by reinforcing the power and the autonomy of the regional and municipal bodies and "the circles."

Echenique notes: (1) that the circles are Podemos' "feet on the street and roots in the earth"; and (2) the circles need a clearer role in the organization, which had not yet been fully achieved. He addresses the need for opening debate on "the powers of the Secretaries General and Citizens Councils; on questions of legal form; on the formal relationship between the autonomous *circulos* and the elected bodies (of party alliances and government); as well as on the character of primary systems for the elections of those (political party) bodies; and on the outfitting of electoral lists." Further, Enchenique cautions: "until we know whether there will be (June general) elections or not, we are in a holding pattern...before holding such an Assembly."

- On 6 April, Iglesias claims that Podemos' proposals for a guaranteed annual income for families below the poverty level are "met with mobility" in negotiations with PSOE. As a result, he announces that Podemos will consult with its party base of 370,000 members in a referendum to take place between 14 and 16 April, wherein the questions will be posed: Whether the Party should support a government led by PSOE and Ciudadanos, or a "Government of Change" made up mainly of Socialists and Podemos and its Popular Unity/IU allies?

14

From Prefigurative Movement to Confluence and Electoral Politics

Deep and fast sociopolitical changes are currently taking place in the Indignados movement in Spain. They are singular and unique in Spain's recent and short democratic history. The singularity of the Indignados as a prefigurative social movement mostly relies on the following features:

(1) The success of the Indignados protests "occupying" public institutions has been manifested in:

(a) using the democratic and legal electoral rules and procedures; and

(b) disregarding traditional parties for their own representatives in the local and regional plenaries or the national and European parliaments.[31]

(2) The strong and effective emergence of informal civil networks – many organizing from Internet ICTs and social media – merges with structured social movements and heterogeneous political actors with extensive experience in the fight for social rights. This merging or Popular Unity Platform "formula" is proving to be very effective for political action.

(3) There is high social support (critical social mass) and citizens' trust regarding groundwork activism nearly unknown for the general public. It is a public with long experience in the struggle for civil rights, albeit now with a new generation of citizens' representatives. Particularly, it is worth noting the strong female

leadership dimension.[32]

(4) The focus is on a "program approach" with socially oriented initiatives mainly focused on "emergency social measures" and "democratic regeneration" in institutional, political, and social life. These initiatives are characterized by their rhizomic and transversal nature based on values and a vision of reciprocal solidarity. They target a wide range and layering of social groups in their multiscalar character – from the neighborhood level to the provincial to the national to the European. These are newly formed expressive groups which have been impoverished during the last years of economic crisis and austerity measures. There is a concerted effort to shift from business-oriented politics – seen as one of the main sources of corruption and social distrust of public institutions – to a citizens' needs orientation, i.e. to the reinforcement of compromise and ties with citizens.

(5) There is an avoidance of the Indignados' explicit identification with political or ideological orientations – e.g. in the left/right-wing ideological axis. Decisive is their self-definition as autonomous "popular movements" rather than political parties. Here once more we see the influence of Ernesto Laclau's formulation of a Left Populism as an "empty signifier." Also there is an anti-essentialist post-Marxism in play, showing the influence of Chantal Mouffe's argument (2013) that transformative change can come from within an existing social order.

(6) There is a search for a reconstituted social democratic normativity attentive to the center-oriented ideological values of the middle classes, insufficiently unattended to by the PSOE.

(7) The interpretation of present institutional and democratic structures has a double dimension:

(a) the historical context (from the Second Republic to Franco's dictatorship regime and the transition to democracy); and

(b) the transnational context of cross-border power-centers (financial markets and the European Union's institutions).

(8) There has evolved strong and creative leadership of the citizens' platforms:

(a) taking the initiative in massive street protest and at the polling place;

(b) emerging in political parties like Podemos and Popular Unity to change the socio-economic conditions, rather than performing tactically within the divided-up bureaucracies and public resources of the establishment (*La Casta*).

(9) With all this, there has evolved a new pattern and a new intersubjective sensibility in the relationship between citizens and politics. This is characterized as horizontal, bottom-up, participatory, heterarchical, and continuous. In sum, more democratic decision-making processes grounded in the processes of assemblies – "circles" as the Indignados call them.

(10) The creativity within Spanish civil society heralds its high adaptability and resilient capacity to develop upward-oriented social pacts to manage stressful socio-economic conditions and fast-changing political reordering. It manifests a pragmatic "know-how" based on innovation, flexibility, and skills at building consensual coalitions.

(11) These changes are mostly driven by urban populations

(municipalities over 50,000 inhabitants), underemployed and unemployed well-educated youth, young professionals in the private sector, and civil servants from areas such as education, health, and social services.

There follows a tendency toward the Confluence of new successful socially oriented parties and initiatives into "popular unity candidatures"; the rejection of older political labels or excessive leadership-oriented initiatives.

(1) We move from the confluent flowing of tides of social pacting from below to the electoral weaving together of a meshwork of reconstituted social and political space, not hijacked by the predominant PP-PSOE political class and incorporated into the uncompleted Transition State apparata.

(2) The Transition needs to be taken to a second stage where there is constituted consensual space for establishing norms to sustain a new resilient social pacting – resetting what Felipe González once referred to as a new common ground as a "We": for a shared destiny in actualizing a democratic Spain. How can a democratic Spain be one where its citizens conceive of themselves as members of a community of fate? The political sociologist Ramón Cotarelo (2015) understands this not as a Second Transition, but as a regenerated democratic agenda in the spirit of the First.

(3) This would involve exceeding and surpassing the extent to which the Transition State is insulated from democratic participation. Thus, it is an effort to make state institutions and the political economy more inclusive.

(4) Electoral politics is oriented toward governance – stewardship to pilot, to steer. Well-established political science understands this as the making of rules and standards. This we do by enforcing the rules and standards with sanctions for the purpose of regulating conflicts; for authoritatively allocating resources and values; for securing and improving the delivery of social services; and for steering institutional steady-state adaptation and change. Governance in the vision of Los Indignados amounts to a *"learning sovereign" assembled in autonomous deliberative public spaces.* Governance in this second stage of the Transition State involves responsively coordinating trust networks crossing an outdated civil society–state divide. Cross-border networks need to be held together as responsible and accountable actors in confronting and managing risk in an interdependent and cooperative manner.

(5) The new form of resilient social pacting is one understood as *a decentered mutual stakeholder social pact* – based on the legal practice known as the "frame agreement": that is, a common protocol of standards focused around how mutual learning and a succession of tasks are based for continued negotiated rule-making and rule-enforcing. The underlying concept here comes from video compression technology wherein an image is established as a base, and subsequent images are stored only as changes from the base.

(6) Rather than a state-initiated concertation, which Nancy Bermeo (1994) reviews as a developmental sequencing in the 1980s Transition State, the new social pacting from below is purely civil society initiated – within their own general assemblies for pooling common efforts

and information (*en Común*); for bootstrapping across multiple scales; and for mutually setting standards and enforceable triggered sanctions.

(7) This envisions a remaking of the Transition State within a framework of knowledge, understanding an emergent politics of a more polycentric complexity. This is one that stresses decentered social insertion and mutual monitoring, rather than command and control. More specifically, this amounts to the emergence of:

(a) what the legal scholar Julia Black (2001) characterizes as a *decentering cooperative risk co-regulation* – a more heterarchical and horizontal growth in normative ordering than the more traditional statist monopoly in risk regulation; and

(b) what socio-economics labels as the *sustainable community movement organizations* (SCMOs) of a *sharing economy*.

(8) In guiding Podemos' electoral strategy and negotiations about entering a coalition government, Iñigo Errejón pursues a Gramscian concept of counter-hegemony ⊚ counterposing transversal cooperative communities against the command and control model Transition State. He envisions a social insertion alongside and within the state. He understands Los Indignados as a movement from social indignation protest that has evolved into the social insertion politics of building an effective electoral war machine aimed at entering the cabinet room of the Moncloa Palace by 2016.

(9) Mayor Manuela Carmena of the *Ahora Madrid* Tides takes a more pragmatic and "flexible approach" in supporting Sánchez's efforts to form a new Government of Change, understanding that the key is less conquering

state power than assuring that the decisions of the assemblies (the circles) are sustained as guides for electoral representatives. The tides of social insertion are understood as the new form and frame of a social governance greater than the representative and executive political governance.

(10) The platforms of Podemos and Popular Unity articulate as objectives the facilitating of public discourse to set the rules of the game, the mode of striving for the constant improvement of infrastructure and quality of life, and the encouraging of the creative expression of entrepreneurship.

(11) In Barcelona in April 2016, Mayor Ada Colau presents a balanced municipal government budget. While adding only 5.7 million euros for social rights, most of the budget is earmarked to pay arrears in city workers' pay; to finance public transport; constructing and reconstructing infrastructure; bailing out a municipal company under indictment; to rescue public gyms previously managed by and left ill-maintained under concession by private companies; and then there is paying for maintenance of public roads, lighting, paving, and signage. To recall Max Weber, yes, governance is the slow boring of hard boards. Colau, like Carmena, has proved to be a serious, pragmatic, and incorruptible public servant and leader.

(12) Contrary to the thesis of Simon Tormey in his 2015 book *The End of Representative Politics*, Los Indignados has proven to be more than the expression of the unmediated politics of occupation, initiation, and affinity groups. Los Indignados is an imaginative challenge to the model of the state sustained by well-meaning social democratic

elites and trade union leaders in a so-called golden age of the 1970s. It is an attempt to actualize the Transition to a democratic Spain.

15

A Movement Left Party

The contentious politics of a social movement engenders a new "frame" wherein citizens constitute a new theme in the public agenda, expressively creating alternative symbolic spaces for change (Oñate, 2013; McAdam and Tarrow, 2010, 2011; Snow, 2004). The street demonstrations triggered by the Indignados movement crystallize into all sorts of hybridized and transversal forms where Podemos circles and 15-M assemblies overlap, overlay, or metamorphosize. Podemos seeks to embody the *15 mayismo* outrage and spiritedness to disentangle, elucidate, and sort out political inclusion possibilities for purposes of mobilization (Calvo and Àlvarez, 2015).

Podemos relies on its efficient interpretation of public participation codes, mobilization networks, and discursive opportunities that are the legacy of the Indignados (Flesher-Fominaya, 2014; Martín, 2015; Subirats, 2015a: 126–8; Subarits, 2015b). This new party's pragmatic and tactical realism adapts to a fast-changing sociopolitical environment without attempting to satisfy all identity and ideological preferences (see Klandemans, 2004). Indeed, in working on Popular Unity electoral alliances during the May 2015 local and regional elections, Podemos understood the autonomous rights of municipal horizontal and participatory decision-making to engage in their own respective direct collective action, seeking to actualize public goods (Martín, 2015).

Podemos leaders like Errejón are motivated by the search for such a wider hybridized and heterogeneous audience. They apply what the post-Marxist radical democrat Ernesto Laclau (1999: 36–46) referred to as seemingly non-ideological *empty signifiers*. Such a signifier absorbs more of what we want to impose on it than what it emits in terms of meaning – for example, "social justice," "precariousness," "the environment," "La Casta." In mobilizing voters, Podemos confronts the vicious circle. In its quest to create an alternative democratic culture, must it inevitably slide into reproducing the organizational practices from the old politics? Does it keep acting as a tribune of the people, or as a pressure group? Or does it attempt to assume institutional responsibility? (Terranova, 2011: 119).

Political sociology designates a political party like Podemos as a "movement party" (Kitschelt, 2006). However, what may very well be more appropriate is the term "movement Left party." This conceptual distinction refers in a resonant manner to the Bolivian party known as Movement toward Socialism (MAS) in this new century. The conceptual insight is used by Levitsky and Roberts (2011: 11–16). MAS and Podemos are distinct from *populist Left* parties like that of Chavez in Venezuela or Correa in Ecuador, in that the organization for power between party and movement is dispersed rather than concentrated. The organization is grounded in a fluid constellation of autonomous movements. They succinctly provide an ideal typical definition (Levitsky and Roberts, 2011: 15) of a movement Left party and its context "where autonomous social and political movements enter the political arena to create a partisan vehicle of their own to contest state power."

This movement Left party politics is unlike the *personalismo* and concentrated power of the populist Left, and the concentrated institutionalized populist machine politics of the Peronistas in Argentina. It is a new form of political party organization whose internal structures disperse power among self-mobilized grassroots actors with their bottom-up mobilizing dynamic. Further, party leaders are more likely to be held accountable by the base. While the relation between party and movements is dispersed like the *institutionalized partisan mass party Left* in Chile, Uruguay, and Brazil, the movement Left eschews their emphasis on professionalism. Again to cite Levitsky and Roberts (op. cit.), *the movement Left party* represents the emergence of a new political force that displaces traditional party organization. Unlike the populist Left its leadership is directly spawned by popular movements organized outside the electoral arena.

Bolivia from 1985 through 2003 was a model of neoliberal reform focused on stability in controlling hyperinflation. But its *democracia pactada* became saddled with clientelism and corruption, and was in need of renewal. A familiar sequence of events. Evo Morales' leadership of MAS was to be grounded in an extensive network of peasant unions and organizations of indigenous peoples. In the 1980s, MAS was preceded by another decentered confederation, *La Asemblea Soberana de los Pueblos* (Sovereign Assembly of the Towns). Morales is institutionally constrained in MAS to hear alternative points of view, and to experience contestation. He is constrained from incarnating any undifferentiated and homogenized "will of the People" (see Oikonomakis and Espinoza, in Stahler-Sholk et al., eds, 2014: 285–307).

Why this Bolivian interlude? In 2011, Iñigo Errejón completed his 2011 doctorate in recent Bolivian populism. His focus was on the movement Left radical democracy and its parallels with Laclau's theorizing – not on Chavez's Left populism as foes of Podemos often allege.

Podemos started rumination and debate on whether political parties would explicitly manifest their pacting intentions before the election results, or what parties should ask their affiliates in possible post-electoral pacts. Significantly, many autonomous movements and community movement organizations do not want to be absorbed by Podemos – which they see as merely a political vehicle that does not represent the diversity of Indignados' spiritedness.

Juan Carlos Monedero (*El Diario*, 1 June 2016) characterizes Podemos as follows: "We are a party whose success is to deny itself" ("Podemos es un partido cuyo éxito es negarse a sí mismo").

The Indignados and its political vehicle are more than the habituated *personalismo* of Iglesias playing with floating empty signifiers as a spectacle on cable TV shows like *La Tuerka* and *Fort Apache*. It is more than a play of signs, discourse, and ideals. The Indignados embodies mutually experienced relations of practice. And as E.P. Thompson (1979: 166–7) reminds us, these are experienced relations treating history as "unmastered practice," a movement of reflexive mediations as Touraine would understand them. These are forms of transversal relations of "thick practices" (e.g. SCMOs, resilient social pacting). And the frames they employ vary independently of what they are of; they are more than their objects of meaningful reference.

The movement relations of practices are not seen as moldable into a specific institutional fixity; they are understood as resistant to centralizing vertical integration, as a continuing instrumentality: an efficient electoral machine. Contrarily, the movement Left party for the Indignados looks more like a reversed pyramid – one that emphasizes sustaining a new sociopolitical ethos of working together in a common cause centrifugally and heterarchically.

Already at the founding Vistalegre constituent congress in October 2014, Iglesias and his Claro Que Podemos faction succeeded in installing a vertical General Secretariat model with hierarchically controlled closed lists for internal primaries, rather than open lists. Further, the vertical integration partisan party leadership tactics of Iglesias and Errejón – both inside Parliament and outside – stirred charges of a different dimension of mistrust: an arrogance of power. This is an arrogance of overweening confidence that was becoming more than audacious assertion; it bordered on overbearing conceit and self-reference in considering each of their acts as "historical moments."

In contrast, the examples of Ada Colau, Manuela Carmena, and Mónica Oltra radiated humility rather than swag.

Recognizing this recurring sense of the de-legitimation of the Podemos leadership, Iglesias would announce by the end of March 2016 that – in talks on constituting a coalition government with PSOE – he was removing himself from consideration of a ministerial role. Then, he turned to Pablo Echenique – a leader of the Sumando Podemos minority faction – to restore the participation in and energy of the horizontal democracy of the *circulos*. Walter Benjamin once noted that revolution is not a runaway train of exuberance, that the application of the emergency brake is important every now and then.

So, to unfold the open-ended concept of a movement Left party, we can note from the reflexively mediating experience and praxis of Podemos in association with the autonomous movement associations of the Indignados:

(1) not an advocacy of statist control or coordination of a stabilizing concertation, but an increased emphasis on sustainable community movement organizations (SCMOs);

(2) not a maintaining of an insulated space of the political, but an opening up of a new sociopolitical ecology of critical spaces with an emphasis on local candidatures and municipalism;

(3) an emphasis on a society of autonomous subjects capable of constituting themselves as Social Subjects of Rights articulating a new understanding of the self-reference of polity;

4) more of a sense of a stakeholder society with a sense of shared responsibility in adapting to managing risks in an age of increased vulnerability, e.g. in cooperatives, in mutually owned enterprises, in new types of financial services and credit unions; and

(5) recognition that democracy is always incomplete, always contingent.

16

Epilogue

We have studied the Indignados as a new form of mediating politics with a distinct framework of knowledge, set on developing new critical spaces and leveraging institutional presence. In so doing, we have encountered a persistent motif in post-Franco Spain – *transitions anchored in pacts*, of two sorts. There are traditional elite negotiated political pacts. Then, there are social pacts to scale up local initiatives. The social pacts are practical accomplishments in self-organizing governance by social partners engaging each other on a more urban or regional level. They are trusting relationships that can be understood as a supportive habitus of commitments to mutual learning. Embodied in tides of social insertion, they mark a transition to a more complex democracy in Spain, wherein legitimation claims augur and assert what is defined as "common" in the self-reference of the Transition State. This involves extra-parliamentary sustainable community movement organizations (SCMOs) with the potential of being scaled up as social economic councils to coordinate national policy-making.

The Spanish peoples moved on to a second general election on 26 June (26-J), after a failed period of political pacting. With the Podemos alliance's 69 deputies to Congress and the support of smaller Popular Unity, Catalan, and Basque parties, it might have been possible for PSOE to cobble together a small but workable progressive minority government. The Sánchez-led PSOE wanted to govern with Podemos alliance support, but not to include its leaders in government with any ministerial posts.

As April approached – and with his second attempt at investiture foiled, if not bungled – Sánchez even sought to stir up internal tensions within Podemos. Sánchez hinted that Iglesias' number two, Iñigo Errejón, was partial to supporting a coalition with a Sánchez-led government, as was Manuela Carmena. He inferred that Pablo Echenique was leapfrogged over Errejón to number two – purportedly to re-energize the grassroots *circulos* (assemblies) – as a tilt to Podemos hardliners like Juan Carlos Monedero and Teresa Rodríguez.

Sánchez does not want to implement a large part of the Podemos alliance platform. This is not just due to his resistance to greater autonomy to the regions, especially the Basques and the Catalans. PSOE leadership linkages to Spain's corporate elites weigh heavily in discouraging Podemos' entry into government. Further, Sánchez tied his own hands in seeking investiture as Prime Minister by forming a coalition with Ciudadanos, a neoliberal-oriented partner whom the Podemos alliance would never support. The Podemos leader exclaimed: "You cannot look Left for a social agreement and to the Right for an economic agreement."

Iglesias' frailty is his occasional arrogance, off-putting enough to be scorned by Colau, Carmena, and Mónica Oltra – the Compromís vice-president of the Valencian regional government (Generalitat Valenciana). Throughout April, Iglesias constantly championed the model of the "Pact to the Valencians" – "to the Valencians" was a constant refrain. In one meeting with Sánchez, the press counted Iglesias' usage of the term 30 times as the Podemos leader hailed the promise of Confluence. Sánchez referred to the Valencian Covenant Model more as "ideological miscegenation." In the first week, Oltra and Valencia President Xima Puig (of the PSOE) sat in the visitors' gallery of the Congress of Deputies in Madrid to accentuate the Valencian Left Model. By 26 April, Iglesias sighed that he could not get Sánchez to accept *un Gobierno a la Valenciana*.

Ironically, Iglesias had not originally supported the proposed Valencian Covenant wherein Podemos joined with Compromís and PSOE to form a government for Valencia with Puig as

President and Oltra as Vice President, with the more moderate conciliatory brokering of Valencia Podemos leader Antonio Montiel. Legend has it that the climactic moment came when Oltra whispered to Puig, "Trust me." The five-point Covenant is also known as the tripartite *Pacte Botànic* (Acuerdo del Botánic) signed in Valencia's Botanical Gardens on 11 June 2015. The five principles include: democratic regeneration; rescue of citizens evicted or in need of debt relief; recovery of public control of utilities; a changed model for production; and a new model for funding regional autonomous communities.

By 2 May, the last day to constitute a government, Sánchez informs King Felipe VI that he cannot. The next day the king announces a general election on 26 June. A week later on 9 May, Iglesias and Alberto Garzón, leader of Izquierda Unida (IU) and Unidad Popular (UP), announce a Joint List electoral alliance to leverage a system heavily oriented toward representing the provinces to their mutual advantage. The electoral alliance is called *Unidos Podemos* (United We Can). This could mean increasing their total vote up to 24 or 25% – with a third of the votes of those aged 18 to 55. This would mean surpassing PSOE as the leading party of the Left (popularly labeled *el sorpasso*). Unidos Podemos is targeting 80 to 84 seats so as to seek a workable progressive government. For some (including Gaspard Llamazares of Izquierda Unida), Iglesias is portrayed as a Machiavellian bent on pushing out PSOE and extinguishing IU, while waiting to topple a Popular Party/Ciudadanos government in the next general election.

The Joint List was to work on a 6:1 ratio; IU/UP gets every sixth position on the proportional representation electoral list. Alberto Garzón yields the top spots to Iglesias, Echenique, and Errejón. Again in the alliance are Colau's En Comú Podem in Catalonia, Oltra's Compromís – Podemos-EUPV a la Valenciana, En Marea compuesto por Podemos in Galicia, Equo, Left Batzarre-Assembly Navarra, the Asturian Left, the Segoviemos,

Democracia Participativa, Building Left/Socialist Alternative... among others in the soup of acronyms. By the close of May, Ahora Madrid announces it will work for the Unidos Podemos Joint List, abandoning its impartiality in the 20 December election campaign – while respecting Madrid Mayor Carmena's decision to stay out of any campaigning.

Polls showed that Unidos Podemos could win anywhere from 84 to 95 seats. Exit polls confirmed this as the vote count started that Sunday evening of 26-J. Even one hour into the count, analysts and pundits were talking 90 or more seats. But within a few hours, disappointment ensued that started to turn into agony.

Rajoy's PP was increasing his share of the vote by 4% and adding 14 seats. PP's total vote: 7,906,185 (137 seats). *Sorpasso* was not achieved, even though PSOE was having its worst showing since the Transition State was constituted: 22.7% of the vote (down to 5,424,709), and a fall of five seats in the Congress to 85. Ciudadanos lost 1% (but had a total of 3,123,769), falling to 13% overall and losing eight seats to PP. Unidos Podemos as a strategy seemed to have failed, even backfired, as together, Podemos and Izquierda Unida lost 1.1 million votes, yet together they held on to the 71 deputy seats they had won in the 20 December general election. The Unidos Podemos Confluence reached 5,049,734 and came out as follows:

Party	Votes	Seats
Podemos-IU-Equo	3,201,170	45 seats (+1)
En Comú Podem	848,526	12 seats (no change)
Compromís-Podemos-EUPV	655,895	9 seats (no change)
In Tide (En Marea-Podemos-Anova-EU)	344,143	5 seats (-1)

Catalonian Republican Left (ERC-CatSi) at 629,294 held on to nine seats, while Catalonian conservative CDC at 481,839 held on to eight seats. Basque Nationalist EAJ-PNV at 286,215 held firm, but fell from six to five seats. EH Bildu as the other Basque Party held on to their two seats. The Canary Island Nationalists held on to their one seat. The 26 Nationalist deputies potentially hold the balance of power, as there is loathing about yet a third general election by December. Interestingly, Unidos Podemos scores well in these regions: Basque Country at 29.05%; Navarra at 28.33%; Balear Islands at 25.38%; Valencia at 25.37%; Catalonia at 24.51%; and notably in Asturias at 23.78%; Galicia at 22.18%; Madrid at 21.23%; Canary Islands at 20.24%.

- Rajoy could form a minority government with PSOE abstention or even a Grand Coalition on the model of Merkel's CDU/CSU and Gabriel's SPD in Germany: either of these moves could lead to further deterioration of PSOE and are moves Sánchez rejects.
- Rajoy could cobble together 176 deputies in a government with Ciudadanos and some conservative Nationalists, but Albert Rivera says only on condition that Rajoy is no longer Prime Minister.
- Sánchez can finally put together his coalition with the help of the Catalonian vote, as Iglesias conceded to this idea late that Sunday night. But after a week, Sánchez had not returned Iglesias' call, and rubbished the Podemos leader that Sunday night for being arrogant and not negotiating in good faith ever to form a government in March and April.
- While Podemos held to some minimalist hope for a role in government, by the end of a week they declared they were prepared to serve as an opposition party and prepare for government in the near future.

The issue confronting PSOE is how to confront the urban transformation: the interweaving of urban spaces and interurban networks that marks the renewed democratic transition. The cities are the launching pads of the Indignados and their remaking of social space. Podemos and its Confluence partners are very much the political party of this eruption and transformation. Izquierda Unida focuses more on a post-neoliberal political economy: opening up the fiscal space that has been choked off by austerity policies; nudging Podemos back toward debt relief and something like the basic income guarantee; putting into effect community jobs/public works programs; and getting beyond an impaired Eurozone structure. These political economy policies have been detailed by Eduardo Garzón, the chief economist for Unidad Popular and Alberto's brother.

The aftershocks of this second and more extensive democratization movement in Spain are affecting both PP and PSOE internally. Within each party, there are calls for a more popular way of choosing the next leader. The eruption and transformation from the cities has resulted from the realization that neither states nor markets have been successful in systemically delivering public goods like housing and jobs, or common goods like health and environmental sustainability. Central government will increasingly need to look to approaches of a more bottom-up and decentered character to satisfy developmental needs, to the new interurban local spaces into which investment is channeled. The Transition State form will need to be adapted so as to deal with the fact that there are a multiplicity of political authorities at different levels and in different registers. The state form will have to be adapted to complement the development of solidarity economies. The parties of the Left will have to learn to work together as a "responsible Left" in a spirit of Confluence in grinding out a mutually debated and constituted self-referential sense of "the common" without thought of extinguishing or blocking one another.

The rise of Podemos has been so fast – two years – that its

assumed momentum became infectious, even leading pollsters to overestimate their strength. Again to quote Errejón, Podemos has been so on the run-up that they have scarcely tied their shoelaces. Still, their two-year surge has both channeled Indignados into a stable national electoral force as the third party with 21–24% of the vote, breathing down the neck of PSOE. Their surge may have crested for a while, yet they have not lost seats in 26-J. They remain a presence, a habitus for creative social insertion.

Podemos was born to give political expression as an anti-establishment movement Left party of the new generation, as well as a force to movement beyond the 1978 Transition State form. It is also a breakthrough to a twenty-first-century politics beyond Spanish traditions of patron-client practices. Along the way, though, the new party – as Mayors Colau and Carmena infer – has neglected its connection to the tides of social insertion and the associated sustainable community movement organizations of a sharing economy. The 1.1 million drop in vote is tied to what Carolina Bescansa detects is a *demobilization*: probably many young voters frustrated with Iglesias' parliamentary antics and scheming; also many IU voters who resist their party being swallowed up by Podemos. A million votes were lost to traditional parties. Why? How?

Brexit – Friday 24 June 2016

Two days before 26-J, the Spanish stock exchange (IBEX) crashed, as the aftershocks of the British referendum vote to leave the European Union had traumatic aftershocks throughout global financial markets. Rajoy immediately went on the airwaves to urge calm and point to the stability and recovery his austerity policies had led to – reducing unemployment by 5% and making Spain one of the fastest-growing economies in the Eurozone. No mention that his Interior Minister was indicted days before, and that his Treasurer was in jail. Rajoy immediately planted the seeds of fear: of the danger of the populism that led to Brexit;

of how populism causes instability and uncertainty; of how referenda such as those demanded by autonomous regions – as new states – were dangerous. Iglesias attempts to give a patriotic speech in response. The Saturday before election-day Sunday is a "day of reflection" where campaigning is banned. It was now also a day of heightened anxiety and uncertainty just before voting. Unidos Podemos' message of change was also seen as a source of fear. The memory of the unstable Popular Front of the Second Republic was being evoked.

In the enthusiasm for Podemos' surge, some key matters were being neglected. There is the perception that Iglesias was trying to sabotage Sánchez's good faith effort to create a post 20-D government. This is coupled with Iglesias' disagreement with Errejón about this, leading to the purge of Errejón ally Sergio Pascual – as secretary of territorial organization. His replacement by Sumando Podemos ultra Echenique had a strong scent of Leninist tactics. This in a country where memories of the role of the communists (*los rojos*) in the Civil War still generates shudders.

By April, Podemos had dropped to 13% in the polls as Iglesias' scheming was definitely hurting. How well the pact with Garzón's IU actually helped is still to be discerned, as they rallied to 21% in two months. There was discontent within Podemos between the Pablistas and the Errejonistas. Errejón continued with a Laclau-driven message of the floating empty signifier of populist reasoning, detached from traditional leftist rhetoric or style. This was seen as more attractive to the young and the swing vote of the insecure middle-aged. The older voters were sticking to the traditional parties; even the poor of Andalucía continued to depend on the PSOE machine politics of local welfare.

Errejón continued to preach the *transversality* of a new progressive alliance – Confluence as a constellation of progressive parties – across the layers, across the scales, flowing deep and flowing wide. And not a more traditional identification with the Left.

At times, Errejón talks of a new social democracy for the twenty-first century – a position Iglesias increasingly took in the May and June run-up to 26-J: the basic guaranteed income; a solidarity tax on the financial sector; reversal of cuts in health and education; reinstatement of collective bargaining rights; a ban on utilities from cutting off poor people; defending social rights; protecting the potentially homeless from eviction; reimposing rent controls.

Our book ends as it begins – with the book cover image of Errejón and the other very young and pluri-national Indignados now as legislators for tomorrow in the Parliament situated in Castile. Errejón makes their fervent appeal and implores the old regime to make the needed changes in re-embedding "the social" and changing the state form. Party secretary of political and social analysis/Complutense professor of political sociology and methodology Carolina Bescansa cradles her baby while she participates in both her science and politics as vocations.

The Indignados are a generational and a pluri-national insurgency criticizing the political class, the financiers, and the corrupt traditional political parties rather than blaming immigrants. They seek a pluri-national confederation of states, in a new national state form of autonomous state forms of the "peoples of Spain," perhaps a United Kingdom of Spain. Some pollsters and pundits foresee Ada Colau of Barcelona as the prime minister who will soon usher in that transition.

17

Afterword

by Ramón Cotarelo

If the "Indignados" movements succeed, they would have quite a task renewing the old ways of the traditional political system from a new more radically minded democratic standpoint. If they don't, they will have to adapt to this very same existing system. They will have to get *institutionalized*, that is, as the New Left once put it, "make its long march through the institutions." Such is namely the case with Podemos as far as it claims to be a political delegate and executor of the Indignados mandate.

Podemos sees itself as a political party, although a *new model* one: on the one hand a party along classical lines, and on the other a kind of front organization, encompassing other spontaneous organizations which have sprouted out in different parts of the country. Some of them show a spirit of *grassroots politics*, whereas others have more specific goals. And all together make out the *confluences* with which Podemos makes its stand at the ballots. The Spanish electoral law allows for coalitions to be formed, so-called "instrumental parties" (*partidos instrumentales*), in order to catch more votes. Podemos articulates therefore a variety of autonomous movements. Here dawns a "new politics" idea geared to put an end to the two-party system and question the traditional party politics.

The outcome of the local councils and autonomic elections of 2015 seems to validate such a conclusion as the so-called "emergent forces" made a breakthrough in the institutions. According to the "New Politics" blueprint, these institutions are managed today by conglomerates of organizations which challenge the old patterns of party coalitions. The cases of Madrid and Barcelona are often cited, along with other examples of smaller town councils, like Valencia, Cádiz, or A Coruña. To repeat: we deal here mainly with municipal politics. In the autonomic elections all parties put forward their own name, although in certain cases, the *confluences*, they also make a bid in the electoral contests.

On considering with greater detail these confluences, we cannot overlook the fact that they have a variable relationship with the national question. In contemporary Spanish politics there is the usual left/right cleavage along with the national/ plurinational one. Accordingly the theory of the confluences seen as clusters of spontaneous social movements doesn't explain satisfactorily the facts, unless the national question be taken into account.

In the most significant municipalities, the game is played by the old-style political parties along with the emergent one, Podemos. If any alternative social movement takes a stand in local government it will surely show different degrees of nationalist or pro-independence leanings. The national question (with different nuances in each of the "historical nationalities") can hardly be considered a typical element of any "New Politics" and will therefore need some kind of explanation.

The issue might be illustrated considering two representative municipalities: Barcelona and Madrid. Barcelona is run by a coalition government led by Barcelona en Comú. Other members of the alliance are ERC and PSC (traditional parties) and, at least externally, the CUP, a grassroots movement. At the Barcelona Confluence, Podemos has a rather modest, unassuming role. Besides, the nationalist discourse of the whole formation is a confusing, if not contradictory one. While ERC and the CUP are openly independentist, the PSC is not, and in Barcelona en Comú many trends coexist, although what seems to predominate we might call the "referendum" line, which is not necessarily pro-independence. Defending people's right to decide, they argue, doesn't turn you automatically into an independence supporter.

Madrid City Council political structure is different and easier to understand because it has no independentist tendencies. The political confrontation is the right/left cleavage. The government is a coalition of Madrid Ahora (the Confluence) and the PSOE. In the opposition, PP and Citizens.

Madrid Ahora, a development of a previous Ganemos Madrid, is inspired by and in close touch with Guanyem Barcelona. Ganemos Madrid comes in association with Podemos, IU, and Equo. The majority of councilors belong to Podemos, but the post of Mayor is held by Manuela Carmena, of Ganemos Madrid.

Although the electoral system is not presidential, the personal nature of the office of Mayor gives this a special relevance. On top of that, both mayoresses, Colau and Carmena, have a strong leadership style which sometimes collides strikingly with the spirit of the Indignados movement.

All factors considered – personal leadership, different "weight" of seats in representative bodies, impact and nature of the national question – municipal politics have a more fragmentary nature than the regional ("autonomic") and national ones. Other smaller municipalities, like Valencia, Cadiz, A Coruña, seem to confirm this conclusion. Such fragmentation reaches a maximum in the local councils where the left/right cleavage overlaps the national/plurinational one.

In the case of Madrid, the *sorpasso* of the PSOE by Podemos in confluence with the old Communists is a fact. Whether or not this confluence gives way to a hegemonic party of the Left in Madrid remains to be seen. At any rate, the task of rebuilding the PSOE to get it back to the moments of glory at the beginning of the Transition looks like a Sisyphus curse.

In the case of Barcelona, the perspectives are different. The national/multinational axis prevails and reflects the polarization – democratic and civilized, but polarization nonetheless – in the whole of Catalan society. For the time being, the Indignados are represented in the Catalan Parliament by the group Catalunya

Sí que es Pot which includes Podemos but not Barcelona en Comú. Things would surely look different if Barcelona en Comú would stand up for the next regional election, in which case there will likely be a merge between the two groups, probably under leadership from Ada Colau of Barcelona en Comú. Whether or not Colau poses her candidacy as president of Catalonia, everything points to the birth of a third option in the independence/no independence axis. *Prima facie* it looks like a good idea. The problem is its feasibility in a highly polarized society.

The impact of the Indignados on municipal politics has deepened their fragmentary nature. But it would be a mistake to conclude from this that the promise of a "new politics" – to include into a single denomination all proposals of Indignados – will lead to a future without problems. It is not clear that its grasp at the micro-level of government will go on to do the same at the meso- and macro-levels.

In fact, municipal politics has always been fragmentary. Their own nature, the close relationships between citizens and administrators, the narrow scope of policy decisions, and the sheer demographic dimensions – all of these offer the possibility of articulating independent, even personalist options. Besides, the relatively low costs of erecting local alternatives make them the more probable. The reservoir of independent options serves as a breeding ground for the emergence of the confluences. Success at the local level drives the platforms in the wake of the Indignados toward higher institutional orders, the regional or national domains. And it is there where the action of the confluences begins to present difficulties because it is not easy to handle representative institutions with radical participatory, horizontal, assembly-like criteria.

By the time the Indignados via Podemos and the confluences push toward the supreme representative and legislative organ of the state, this challenge becomes more acute. Equally risky would be to get into reverse and turn the promise of the "New Politics" into a remake of the "old politics." In its way toward the general ballot of 26 June 2016, Podemos entered into an electoral coalition with *Izquierda Unida* (United Left), an umbrella name for the old Spanish Communist Party. Together they hammered out a new name for the construct, namely *Unidos Podemos* (United We Can), with a somewhat disappointing result of losing more than 1 million votes in comparison with the previous election. It is difficult to see what the old Spanish Communist Party has to do with any "New Politics" approach of the Indignados movement and the confluences. Surely, the Communists sided, individually and as a party, with the Indignados from the very beginning, but always as outsiders, as a kind of external support, with very few points in common.

We need to remember Karl Marx's counsel in *The 18th Brumaire of Louis Bonaparte*. We ought not to let the traditions of dead generations *weigh like a nightmare on the brains of the living* Indignados.

PICTURE 8

President Obama talks with Spanish political opposition leader Pablo
Iglesias Turrión, Secretary General of Podemos, at Torrejón Air Base in
Madrid, 10 July 2016. Courtesy: The White House (Pete Souza)

References

Ainger, Katharine (2013). "In Spain They Are All *Indignados* Nowadays". *Guardian*: 28 April.

Bäckstrand, Karin (2006). "Multistakeholder Partnerships for Sustainable Development: Rethinking Legitimacy, Accountability and Effectiveness". *European Environment* 16: 290–306.

Bauman, Zygmont (2008). *Confianza y temor en la ciudad: vivir con extranjeros*. Arcadia, Barcelona. Originally in (2003) *City of Fears, City of Hopes*. London: Goldsmith's College.

Beckert, Jens (2007). "The Great Transformation of Embeddedness: Karl Polanyi and the New Economic Sociology". MPIfG Discussion Paper 07/1. Cologne: Max Planck Institut für Gesellschaftsforschung.

Bermeo, Nancy (1994). "Sacrifice, Sequence and Strength in Successful Dual Transitions". *The Journal of Politics* 56/3: 601–27.

Bernstein, J.M. (2001). *Adorno: Disenchantment and Ethics*. Cambridge: Cambridge University Press.

Black, Julia (2001). "Decentring Regulation: Understanding the Role of Regulation and Self-Regulation in a 'Post-Regulatory' World". *Current Legal Problems* 54: 103–46.

Block, Fred and Somers, Margaret (1984). "Beyond the Economistic Fallacy: The Holistics Social Science of Karl Polanyi". In Theda Skocpol (ed.), *Vision and Method in Historical Sociology*. Cambridge: Cambridge University Press, pp. 47–84.

Block, Fred and Somers, Margaret (2014). *The Power of Market Fundamentalism: Karl Polanyi's Critique*. Cambridge: Harvard University Press.

Blyth, Mark (2013). *Austerity: The History of a Dangerous Idea*. Oxford: Oxford University Press.

Bookchin, Murray (1977). *The Spanish Anarchists: The Heroic Years, 1968–1936*. New York: Harper & Row Colophon Books.

Bowles, Samuel and Gintis, Herbert (1998). "Is Equality *Passé?*: Homo Reciprocans and the Future of Egalitarian Politics". *Boston Review* 23.

Brenner, Neil (2004). *New State Spaces: Urban Governance and the Rescaling of Statehood*. Oxford: Oxford University Press.

Caliskan, Koray and Michel Callon (2009). "Economization, Part 1: Shifting Attention from the Economy towards Processes of Economization". *Economy and Society* 36: 369–98.

Calvo, Kerman and Álvarez, Iago (2015). "Limitaciones y exclusiones en la institutionalización de la indignación: de 15-M a Podemos", *Revista Española de Sociología* 24: 115–22.

Calzada, Inés and Eloise del Pino (2011). "Are Spaniards Different? European Convergence and Regional Development in the Evaluation of the Welfare State". In Ana Marta Guillén and Margarita Léon (eds), *The Spanish Welfare State in European Context*. Farnham: Ashgate, pp. 139–62.

Castel, Robert (1995). *Metamorphoses de la question sociale*. Paris: Fayard.

Castells, Manuel (1992). *The Informational City: Economic Restructuring and Urban Development*. Oxford: Blackwell.

Castells, Manuel (2012). *Networks of Outrage and Hope: Social Movements in the Internet Age*. Cambridge: Polity.

Castoriadis, Cornelius (1987). *The Imaginary Institution of Society*. Trans. Kathleen Blamey, Cambridge: Polity; originally *L'institution imaginaire de la societé*. Paris: Edition de Seuil, 1975.

Chari, Anita (2016). *A Political Economy of the Senses: Neoliberalism, Reification and Critique*. New York: Columbia University Press.

Connolly, William E. (1987). *Politics and Ambiguity*. Madison: University of Wisconsin Press.

Cotarelo, Ramón (1996). *Transición politica y consolidación democrática. España (1976–1986)*. Madrid: Centro de

Investigaciones Sociológicas.

Cotarelo, Ramón (2011). *Memoria de Franquismo*. Madrid: Akal.

Cotarelo, Ramón and Roca, José Manuel (2015). *La Antitransición: La derecha neofranquista y el saqueo de España*. Valencia: Tirant Humanidades.

Cristi, Renato (1998). *Carl Schmitt and Authoritarian Liberalism: Strong State, Free Economy*. Cardiff: University of Wales Press.

Cruz, Jesus (2011). *The Rise of Middle-Class Culture in Nineteenth-Century Spain*. Baton Rouge: Louisiana State University Press.

Dale, Garth (2010). *Karl Polanyi: The Limits of the Market*. Cambridge: Verso.

DeLanda, Manuel (1997). *A Thousand Years of Non-Linear History*. New York: Zone Books.

DeLanda, Manuel (1998). "Deleuze and the Open-Ended Becoming of the World". Paper presented at the "Chaos/Control/Complexity Conference" at Bielefeld, Germany http://www.cddc.vt.edu/host/delanda/pages/becoming.htm

Deleuze, Gilles (1966/88). *Bergsonism*. Trans. H. Tomlinson and B. Habberjam. New York: Zone Books.

Deleuze, Gilles (1968/93). *Difference and Repetition*. Trans. P. Patton. New York: Columbia University Press.

Deleuze, Gilles (1988/93). *The Fold: Leibniz and the Baroque*. Trans. T. Cooley. Minneapolis: University of Minnesota Press.

Deleuze, Gilles and Felix Guattari (1987). *A Thousand Plateaus*. Trans. B. Mussamu. Minneapolis: University of Minneapolis Press.

Dewey, John (1927/2010). *The Public and Its Problems*. Ed. M.L. Rogers. State College: Penn State University Press.

Dhaliwal, Puneet (2012). "Public Squares and Resistance: The Politics of Space in the Indignados Movement". *Interface* 4/1: 251–73.

Dolgoff, Sam (1971). *Bakunin on Anarchy*. Ed./Trans./Intro. Sam Dolgoff. NewYork: Random House Vintage.

Donzelot, Jacques (1984). *L'invention du social: essai sur le declin des passions politiques*. Paris: Fayard/Éditions du Seuil.

Ebbinghaus, Bernhard (2006). "Reforming Bismarckian Corporatism: The Changing Role in Social Partnership in Continental Europe". Paper presented at the Minda de Gunzburg Center for European Studies at Harvard University.

Eiland, Howard (2001, 8 April). "Reception in Distraction". Paper presented at the "Benjamin Now Symposium: Critical Encounters with Walter Benjamin's Arcades Project" at the Forbes Center for Research in Culture and Media Studies, Brown University.

Eiland, Howard and Michael Jennings (2014). *Walter Benjamin: A Critical Life*. Cambridge: Harvard University Press.

Elias, Norbert (1939/94). *The Civilizing Process: Sociogenetic and Psychogenetic Investigations*. Trans. Edmund Jephcott. Oxford: Blackwell. Comprises *The History of Manners*, Blackwell: 1978; and *State Formation and Civilization*, Blackwell: 1982.

Encarnación, Omar G. (1997). "Social Concertation in Democratic and Market Transitions". *Comparative Political Studies* 30/4: 387–419.

Encarnación, Omar G. (2001). "Civil Society and the Consolidation of Democracy in Spain". *Political Science Quarterly* 116/1: 53–79.

Errejón, Iñigo (2011). "La lucha por la hegemonía durante el primer gobierno del MAS en Bolivia (2006–2009): un analysis discursive." Teçis Doctoral, Universidad Complutense de Madrid. http://eprints.ucm.es/14574/1/T33089.pdf

Errejón, Iñigo (2015). "We the People: El 15-M/un populismo indignado?"*ACME: An International Journal for Critical Geographies* 14/1: 124–56.

Esping-Andersen, Gøsta (1990). *The Three Worlds of Welfare Capitalism*. Cambridge: Polity Press & Princeton: Princeton University Press.

Field, Bonnie N. (2005). "De-Thawing Democracy: The Decline of Political Party Collaboration in Spain (1977-2004),"

Comparative Political Studies, 38:9, 1079-1103.

Field, Bonnie N. (2009). "A Second Transition in Spain?: Policy, Institutions and Interparty Politics under Zapatero (2004-8)," *South European Society and Politics*, 14:4, 79-102.

Fishman, Robert M. (2004). *Democracy's Voices: Social Ties and the Quality of Public Life in Spain*. Ithaca: Cornell University Press.

Fishman, Robert M. (2012). *Working Class Organization and the Return to Democracy in Spain*. Ithaca: Cornell University Press.

Flesher-Fominaya, Cristina (2014). *Social Movements and Globalization: How Protests, Occupations and Uprisings Are Changing the World*. New York: Palgrave Macmillan.

Flesher-Fominaya, Cristina (2015a). "Podemos' March for Change". *Open Democracy* (1 February 2015). http://www.opendemocracy.net

Flesher-Fominaya, Cristina (2015b). "Redefining the Crisis/ Redefining Democracy: Mobilizing for the Right to Housing in Spain's PAH Movement". *South European Society and Politics* 12/ 4: 465–85.

Flesher-Fominaya, Cristina (2015c). "Debunking Spontaneity: Spain's 15-M Indignados as Autonomous Movement". *Social Movement Studies* 14/2: 142–63.

Garud, Raghu and Peter Karnøe (2001). "Path Creation as Mindful Deviation". In R.Garus and P. Karnøe (eds), *Path Dependency and Creation*. Mahwah: Earlbaum.

Gindin, Samuel (2004). "Globalization and Labour: Defining the Problem". Working paper 2004-1: Work in Global Society, McMaster University, 21 January 2004.

Gold, Lorna (2004). *The Sharing Economy: Solidarity Networks Transforming Globalization*. Aldershot: Ashgate.

Gorz, André (1980/82). *Adieux au Proletariat*. Paris: Galilée. / *Farewell to the Working Class*. Trans. Michael Sonenscher. London: Pluto Press.

Gorz, André (1983). *Ecology as Politics*. Trans J. Cloud and P. Viederman. Montreal: Black Rose.

Gorz, André (2010). *Ecologica*. Trans. Chris Turner. Hove, Sussex: Seagull.

Gorz, André (2012). *Capitalism, Socialism, Ecology*. With Chris Turner. London: Verso.

Graeber, David (2002). "The New Anarchists". *New Left Review* 13 (January/February).

Graeber, David (2009). *Direct Action: An Ethnography*. Oakland: AK Press.

Gramsci, Antonio (2011). *Prison Notebooks*, 3 volumes. Trans./Ed. Joseph Buttligies. New York: Columbia University Press.

Guillén, Ana Marta (2010). "Defrosting the Spanish State: The Weight of Conservative Components". Paper presented at the Minda de Gunzburg Center for European Studies, Harvard University; published in Bruno Palier *infra*: 183–206.

Guillén, Ana Marta (2013). "Welfare State under Strain in Southern Europe". *European Journal of Social Security* 17/2: 147–53.

Guillén, Ana Marta and Margarita Léon, eds (2011). *The Consolidation of the Spanish Welfare State*. Farnham: Ashgate.

Gunther, Richard (2009). *The Politics of Spain*. Cambridge: Cambridge University Press.

Gurvitch, Georges (1972). *The Social Frameworks of Knowledge: Explorations in Interpretive Sociology*. Trans. Margaret and Kenneth A. Thompson, New York: Harper and Row.

Habermas, Jürgen (1975). *Legitimation Crisis*. Trans. T. McCarthy. Boston: Beacon.

Habermas, Jürgen (1996). *Between Facts and Norms*. Trans. N. Rehg. Cambridge, MA: MIT.

Harvey, David (2012). *Rebel Cities: From the Right to the City to the Urban Revolution*. London: Verso.

Hemerjick, Anton (2013). *Changing Welfare States*. Oxford: Oxford University Press.

Hessel, Stéphane (2010). *Indignez-vous!* Montpellier: Indigène éditions.

Humblaeck, Carsten (2015). *Spain: Inventing the Nation*. London: Bloomsbury.

Iacoboni, Marco (2009). *Mirroring People: The New Science of How We Connect with Others*. New York: Farrar, Strauss and Giroux.

Iglesias, Pablo (2015). "Understanding Podemos". *New Left Review* 93 (May/June).

Ives, Peter (2005). "Language, Agency and Hegemony: A Gramscian Response to Post-Marxism". *Critical Review of International Social and Political Philosophy* 8/4: 455–88.

Jessop, Bob (2008/14). "Zr relevanz von Luhmann's Systemtheorie und von Laclau und Mouffe's Diskursanalys für die Weiterantwicklung der marxistischen staatstheorie" in J. Hirsch, J. Kannankulam und J. Wissel, eds., Der Staat der bürger-lichen Gesellschaft zum Staatsverständnis von Karl Marx. (Baden-Baden: Nomos, 2008), pp. 157-179. https://bobjessop.org/2014/02/09/the-relevance-of-luhmanns-systems-theory-and-of-laclau-and-mouffes-discourse-analysis-to-the-elaboration-of-marxs-state-theory/

Kassam, Ashifa (2015). "No We Can't?: Podemos Party Comes to Terms with Stagnant Polls". *Guardian*: 15 May.

Kitschelt, Helmut (2006). "Movement Parties". In R. Katz and W. Crotty (eds), *Handbook of Party Politics*. London: Sage.

Kjaer, Poul, and Gúnther Teubner and Alberto Febbrajo, eds (2011). *The Financial Crisis in Constitutional Perspective: The Dark Side of Functional Differentiation*. Oxford: Hart.

Klandesmans, Hans D. (2004). "The Demand and Supply of Participation: Social Psychological Corrolates of Participation in Social Movements". In David A. Snow, Darah A. Soule, and Hans-Peter Kriesi (eds), *The Blackwell Companion to Social Movements*. Oxford: Blackwell.

Laclau, Ernest (1999). "Why Do Empty Signifiers Matter in Politics?" Chapter 6: *Emancipation(s)*. London: Verso: pp. 36–46.

Laclau, Ernesto and Chantal Mouffe (1985). *Hegemony and*

Socialist Strategy. London: Verso.

Latour, Bruno (2005). *Reassembling the Social: An Introduction to Actor-Network Theory*. Oxford: Oxford University Press.

Latour, Bruno (2009). "Spheres and Networks: Two Ways to Reinterpret Globalization". *Harvard Design Magazine*, Harvard School of Design. 30/Spring/Summer: 138–44.

Lawson, Neil (2016). "Social Democracy without Social Democrats: How Can the Left Recover?" *New Statesman*: 12 May.

Lefebvre, Henri (1974). *The Production of Space*. Trans. D. Nicholson-Smith. Oxford: Blackwell.

Lefebvre, Henri (1980). *La revolución urbana*. Madrid: Alianza Editorial.

Lehmbruch, Gerhard (1998, May 30). "Negotiated Democracy, Consociationalism, and Corporatism in German Politics: The Legacy of the Westphalian Peace". Paper presented at the Minda de Gunzburg Center for European Studies, Harvard University.

Levi, Simona (2015). "24-M: It Was Not a Victory for Podemos, but for the 15-M Movement". *Open Democracy* (9 June 2015) http://www.opendemocracy.net

Levitsky, Steven and Kenneth M. Roberts (2011). "Latin America's 'Left Turn': A Framework for Analysis". In Steven Levitsky and Kenneth M. Roberts (eds), *The Resurgence of the Latin American Left*. Baltimore: Johns Hopkins University Press, pp. 1–28.

Lindahl, Hans (2007). "The Paradox of Constituent Power: The Abiguous Self-Constitution of the European Union". *Ratio Juris* 20/4, 485–505.

Lindahl, Hans (2013). *Fault Lines of Globalization*. Oxford: Oxford University Press.

Linz, Juan and Alfred Stepan (1996). *Problems of Democratic Transition and Consolidation*. Baltimore: Johns Hopkins University Press.

Lipset, S. (1981). *Political Man: The Social Bases of Politics*. Garden City: Doubleday.

Lobera, Josep (2015). "De movimientos a partidos: La cristalización electoral de la protesta". *Revista Española de Sociología* 24: 97–105.

Luhmann, Niklas (1979). *Trust and Power*. Trans. H. Davis, J. Roffian, K. Roche. New York: John Wiley.

Luhmann, Niklas (1984). "Staat und Politik: Zur Semantik Selbstbeschreibung politischer Systeme". In U. Bermach (ed.), *Politische Theoringeschichte: Probleme einer Teildisziplin der politischean Wissenschaft*, Opladen: Westdeutscher Verlag.

Luhmann, Niklas (1990a). *Essays on Self-Reference*. Trans. S. Fuchs. New York: Columbia University Press.

Luhmann, Niklas (1990b). *Political Theory in the Welfare State*. Trans. John Bednarz. Berlin: de Gruyter.

Luhmann, Niklas (1992). "The Coding of the Legal System". In A. Febbrajo and G. Teubner (eds), *State, Law, Economy as Autoietic Systems*. Milan: Giuffré, pp. 145–86.

Maeckelbergh, Marianne (2012). "Horizontal Democracy Now: From Alter-Globalization to Occupation". *Interface* 4/1: 207–34.

Maravall, José (1982). *The Transition to Democracy in Spain*. New York: St. Martin's Press.

Marcuse, Peter (2011). "The Purpose of the Occupation Movement and the Fetishizing of Space". *The New Significance*, website, 17 November 2011. http//:www.the new significance.com/ 2011/11/17 peter-marcuse-the-purpose-of –the occupation-movement-and-the fetishizing-of-space

Martín, Irene (2015). "Podemos y otros modelos de partido-movimientos". *Revista Española de Sociología* 24: 107–14.

Martín-Barbero, J. (2009). "La nueva experiencia urbana: trayectos y desconciertos". In *Revista Ciudad Viva*. Junta de Andalucía.

Mathieson, David (2007). *Spanish Steps: Zapatero and the Second*

Transition in Spain. London: Policy Network.

Mattei, Ugo and Bailey, Saki (2013). "Protecting the Commons: Water, Culture and Nature: The Commons Movement in the Italian Struggle against Neoliberal Governance". *South Atlantic Quarterly* 112: 366–77.

McAdam, Douglas and Sidney Tarrow (2010). "Ballots and Barricades: On the Reciprocal Relationships between Elections and Social Movements". *Perspectives on Politics* 81: 525–42.

McAdam, Douglas and Sidney Tarrow (2011). "Movimientos sociales, elecciónes y politica contenciosa: Construyendo puentes conceptuales". In María Jesús Funes (ed.), *A Propósito de Tilly: Conflicto, Poder y Acción Colectiva*. Madrid: Centro de Investigaciones Sociólogicas.

Molinas, César (2013). *Qué hacer con espagña?* Madrid: Ediciones Destinos.

Monedero, Juan Carlos (2011). *La Transición contada a Nuestros Padres: Nocturno de la Democracia Española*. Madrid: Catarata.

Montero, Mercedes (2008). "El miedo al otro en la construcción de las ciudades contemporáneas". In *Revista Sociedad y Utopía* 32. Facultad de Ciencias Políticas y Sociología "León XIII": 173–86.

Moscovici, Serge (2001). *Social Representations: Essays in Social Psychology*. Trans./Ed. G. Duveen. New York: NYU Press.

Mouffe, Chantal (2013). *Agonistics: Thinking the World Politically*. London: Verso.

Nettl, J.P. (1968). "The State as a Conceptual Variable". *World Politics* 20: 559–92.

Offe, Claus (1984). *Contradictions of the Welfare State*. Ed. John Keane. Cambridge: MIT Press.

Offe, Claus (1985). "New Social Movements: Challenging the Boundaries of Institutional Politics". In *Social Research* 52/4: 817–68.

Offe, Claus (2006). "Political Disaffection as the Outcome of Institutional Practices?: Post-Tocquevillian Speculations". In

Mariano Torcal and J.P. Montero (eds), *Political Disaffection in Contemporary Democracies*. London: Routledge.

Offe, Claus (2013). "Europe Entrapped". Cambridge: Polity, 2016. http://www.polity.co.uk/book.asp?ref=9780745687513

Oikonomakis, Leonidas and Fran Espinoza (2014). "Bolivia: MAS and the Movements that Brought It to State Power". In Richard Stahler-Sholk, Harry Vanden and G. D. Knecker (eds), *Rethinking Latin American Social Movements: Radical Action from Below*. Lanham: Rowman and Littlefield, pp. 285–307. Book by Offe containing all this

Oñate, Pablo (2013). "Spanish Citizens' Mobilization in the Early 20th Century: A Framework for the Debate". *Revista Española de Ciencia Política* 33: 31–58.

Ong, Aihwa (2006). *Neoliberalism as Exception: Mutations in Citizenship and Sovereignty*. Durham: Duke University Press.

Ong, Aihwa (2007). "Neoliberalism as a Mobile Technology". *Transactions of the Institute of British Geographers* 32: 3–8.

Ostrom, Elinor (1990). *Governing the Commons: The Evolution of Institutions of Collective Action*. Cambridge: Cambridge University Press.

Ostrom, Elinor and James Walker (2009). "Trust and Reciprocity as Foundations for Cooperation". In Karen Cook, Margaret Levi, and Russell Hardin (eds), *Who Can We Trust?: How Groups, Networks, and Institutions Make Trust Possible*. New York: Russell Sage Foundation.

Pais, Ivana and Giancarlo Provasi (2016). "The Sharing Economy: A Step towards the Re-Embeddedness of the Economy?" (Earlier version: "Re-Embedding the Social: New Models of Production, Critical Consumption and Alternative Lifestyles".) Paper presented at SASE: Society for the Advancement of Socio-Economics Conference: "Moral Economies. Economic Moralities" at University of California, Berkeley, 25 June 2016.

Palier, Bruno, ed. (2008). *A Long Goodbye to Bismarck?: The*

Politics of Welfare Reform in Continental Europe. Amsterdam: Amsterdam University Press.

Payne, Stanley (1993). *Spain's First Democracy: The Second Republic, 1931–36*. Madison: University of Wisconsin Press.

Peck, Jamie and Adam Tickell (2002). "Neoliberalizing Space". *Antipode* 34: 380–404.

Pérez, Sofia (1997). *Banking on Privilege: The Politics of Spanish Financial Reform*. Ithaca: Cornell University Press.

Pérez, Sofia (2016). "Spain's Social Model in the Balance as Parties Attempt to Form a Government". *Open Democracy* (6 March 2016) https://www.opendemocracy.net/can-europe-make-it/sofia-perez/spain-s-social-model-in-balance-as-parties-attempt-to-form-government

Pérez-Diaz, Victor (1993). *The Return of Civil Society and the Emergence of Democratic Spain*. Cambridge: Harvard University Press.

Phillimore, John (2000). "The Limits of Supply Side Social Democracy: Australian Labor, 1983–96". *Politics and Society* 28/4: 557–87.

Piven, Frances Fox (2006). *Challenging Authority: How Ordinary People Change America*. Lanham: Rowman and Littlefield.

Piven, Frances Fox and Richard Cloward (1977). *Poor People's Movements: Why They Succeed, How They Fail*. New York: Atheneum.

Polanyi, Karl (1944). *The Great Transformation: The Political Origins of Our Times*. Boston: Beacon.

Polanyi, Karl (1971). *Primitive, Archaic, and Modern Economies: Essays of Karl Polanyi*. Boston: Beacon.

Rose, Niklas and Peter Miller (2008). *Governing the Present: Administering Economic, Social and Personal Life*. Cambridge: Polity.

Rose, Niklas (1999). *Powers of Freedom: Reframing Political Thought*. Cambridge: Cambridge University Press.

Ross, Carne (2013). *The Leaderless Revolution*. New York: Penguin

Plume.

Royo, Sebastian (2014). "Institutional Degeneration and Economic Crisis: The Case of Spain". Paper presented at the Annual Meeting of the American Political Science Association, Washington, DC.

Sabel, Charles (1994). "Learning by Monitoring: The Institutions of Economic Development". In Neil Smelser and Richard Swedburg (eds), *Handbook of Economic Sociology*. Princeton: Princeton University Press/Russell Sage Foundation.

Sennett, Richard (1970). *The Uses of Disorder: Personal Identity and City Life*. New York: Norton & Company.

Sklar, Martin J. (1988). *The Corporate Reconstruction of American Capitalism, 1890–1916: The Market, the Law, and Politics*. Cambridge: Cambridge University Press.

Snow, David A. (2004). "Framing Process, Ideology and Discursive Fields". In David A. Snow, Sarah Soule, and Hanspeter Kriesi (eds), *The Blackwell Companion to Social Movements*. Oxford: Blackwell.

Soja, Edward W. (1989). *Postmodern Geographies: The Reassertion of Space in Critical Social Theory*. London: Verso.

Standing, Guy (2011). *Precariat: The New Dangerous Class*. London: Bloomsbury Academic Press.

Standing, Guy (2012). "The Precariat: Why It Needs Deliberative Democracy". *Open Democracy* (27 January 2012) http:www. open democracy.net

Stobart, Luke (2014a). "Understanding Podemos (1/3): 15-M and Counter-Politics". *Left Flank* (5 November 2014) http:www. left-flank.org 2014/ 11/ 05

Stobart, Luke (2014b). "Understanding Podemos (2/3): Radical Populism". *Left Flank* (14 November 2014) http:www.left-flank.org 2014/ 11/14

Stobart, Luke (2015a). "Understanding Podemos (3/3): 'Commonsense' Policy". *Left Flank* (2 January 2015) http:// www.left-flank.org 2015/

Stobart, Luke (2015b). "Spain Shows that the 'Anti-Politics' Votes Is Not a Monopoly of the Right". *Guardian*: 28 May.

Streeck, Wolfgang (1992). *Social Institutions and Economic Performance: Studies of Industrial Relations in Advanced Capitalist Societies*. London: Sage.

Streeck, Wolfgang (2011). "The Crisis of Democratic Capitalism". *New Left Review* 71: September/October.

Streeck, Wolfgang (2014). *Buying Time: The Delayed Crisis of Democratic Capitalism*. London: Verso.

Streeck, Wolfgang and Armin Schäfer, eds (2013). *Politics in the Age of Austerity*. Cambridge: Polity.

Subarits, Joan (2015a). "Todo se mueve: Acción colectiva, acción conectiva: Movimientos, partidos e instituciones". *Revista Española de Sociología* 24: 123–31.

Subarits, Joan (2015b). "Desbordar el 'dentro' – 'fuera'?" *Revista Teknokultura* 12/1: 161–8.

Summers, Lawrence H. (1986). "Why Is the Unemployment Rate So Very High Near Full Employment?" *Brookings Papers on Economic Activity* 2: 339–83.

Swyngedouw, Erik (2004). "Globalization or Glocalization?: Networks, Territories and Rescaling". *Cambridge Review of International Affairs* 17: 25–48.

Terranova, Marco (2011). "El Movimiento 15 de Mayo. Hacia un Nuevo proyecto para siglo xxi". In F. Cabal (ed.). *Indignados, 15-M*. Madrid: Mandala Editorial, pp. 118–23.

Thompson, Edward (1979). *The Poverty of Theory and Other Essays*. New York: Monthly Review Press.

Threlfall, Monica (2008). "Reassessing the Role of Civil Society Organizations in the Transition to Democracy in Spain". *Democratization* 15/5: 930–51.

Tilly, Charles (2008). *Contentious Performances*. Cambridge: Cambridge University Press.

Torcal, Mariano (2002). *Disaffected but Democrats: The Origin and Consequences of the Dimensions of Political Support in New*

Latin American and Southern European Democracies. Madrid (manuscript).

Torcal, Mariano and José Ramón Montero (2006). *Political Disaffection in Contemporary Democracies: Social Capital, Institutions, and Politics*. London, Routledge.

Tormey, Simon. (2015). *The End of Representative Politics?* London: Verso.

Torres, Diego (2009). *La crisis financiera: Guía para entenderla y explicarla*. ATTAC.

Touraine, Alain (1977). *The Self-Production of Society*. Trans. Derek Coltman. Chicago: University of Chicago Press.

Touraine, Alain (1981). *The Voice and the Eye*. Trans. Alan Duff. Cambridge: Cambridge University Press.

Touraine, Alain (1988). *The Return of the Actor: Social Theory in Post-Industrial Society*. Trans. Myran Godrich. Minneapolis: University of Minnesota Press.

Touraine, Alain (2009). *Thinking Differently*. Trans. David Macey. Cambridge: Polity.

Walters, William (2004). "Some Critical Notes on 'Governance'". *Studies in Political Economy* 73: 27–46.

Willke, Helmut (2007). *Smart Governance: Governing the Global Knowledge Society*. New York: Campus Verlag/University of Chicago Press.

Yerkes, Mara and Peter Achterberg (2012). *The Transformation of Solidarity: Changing Risks and the Future of the Welfare State*. Amsterdam: Amsterdam University Press.

Endnotes

1. Source: Eurostat. Compare Capgemini y Royal Bank of Canada (RBC) Wealth Management; and Report 2014 from the Spanish Economic and Social Council (Consejo Económico y Social).
2. In the Spanish case based not just on the exponential increment of financial products, but mostly on housing construction.
3. Other official documents, such as the "Report from the commission to the council and the European Parliament" (EU ANTI-CORRUPTION REPORT – Brussels, 3.2.2014, COM (2014) 38 final), shows how "95 percent of Spaniards see corruption as institutionalized," not a surprising figure considering that Spain drops ten places in Transparency International 2013 corruption index. See: http://elpais.com/elpais/2014/02/03/inenglish/1391426403_653818.html
4. While in 2006 the youth unemployment rate in Spain was approximately 17% among those under 25 years old, in 2012 it represented over 50%, being among the highest of the European Union (along with Greece, Portugal, and Italy). Moreover, the unemployment rate among immigrants in 2012 is around 35%, while in 2006 it was just over 12%. Sources: National Statistics and Eurostat.
5. According to the National Statistics Institute (INE), the most vulnerable groups are, in this order, the unemployed (in particular, the long-term unemployed), immigrants, middle-aged Spanish professionals between 41 and 65 years old highly qualified and with work experience, children and young people aged between 18 and 35 years old. Also there are women with dependents under their care (either children or people with disabilities of various kinds, in most cases divorced women with children). And then there are

people on retirement pensions, as well as people living alone – like the elderly, although the latter appear to be showing more resilience to the crisis, at least for the moment. Under this profile, we pay specific attention the group known as the "NEETs" (youth not working or receiving any training), who represent in the European Union approximately 15.4% of the youth, and in Bulgaria, Italy, Ireland, and Spain account for more than one in five young. Source: Eurofound.

6. Since the beginning of the crisis, during the third to the fourth quarter of each year, tens of thousands of public sector jobs have been lost, including 84,000 in 2011 and 36,000 in 2009, while the private sector layoffs have eased.

7. The term "market" has acquired a bad reputation in the media and among the general public. Given the difficulties in identifying the cause or causes of what is happening in the current economic crisis, we can say that this is a bonding concept.

8. Ultimately we are talking about a lack of trust in politicians, democratic institutions, and electoral processes, a rift that is not new, but under current socio-economic conditions we can say that the population has made it explicit. In that sense, actions such as *rodea el congreso* (surround the Congress) intended to make members of Congress feel popular pressure at key moments (such as the approval of the general state budget), but not occupancy of the Congress, an area protected by the Spanish Constitution. In this sense, we could say that with the initiative *rodea el congreso* the Indignados movement defines clear limits on what is to be occupied and not surrounded (the squares and streets), and what is to be surrounded and not occupied (the Congress).

9. With former Rodríguez Zapatero's socialist government 110,000 million euros were provided to private banks between the years 2008 (when the crisis started) and 2011, whereas in 2012 alone the conservative Partido Popular,

currently in power, added 50 billion euros to this figure. Among the arguments justifying these decisions are the need to facilitate the granting of loans to the financial sector (essential for economic recovery), and the threat of an Argentinean *corralito* (December 2001).

10. One of the most tangible achievements of the Indignados movement has been to change the law on mortgages in Spain, even when it's been done only partially.

11. http://www.eldiario.es/catalunya/Entrevista-Ada_Colau-Plataforma_de_Afectados_por_la_Hipoteca-desahucios-ILP_hipotecaria_0_69643131.html

12. It is noteworthy that although the economic crisis has initially struck the low-skilled working class as far as unemployment is concerned (the construction sector and the sectors that depend on it have been the main exponent), this social group is not especially concerned by social demonstrations in the streets and squares of the country.

13. In the context of societies with settled social democratic values, we can talk of a pattern applicable to many other social causes that relate to basic and general rights, with action or activism as something more common among young people or people directly affected by an injustice bounded in time, space, and theme, while larger groups of people can show sympathy or moral support for these causes.

14. One of the platforms structuring the outrage and protests on the Internet is *Democracia Real Ya* (Real Democracy Now), along with many others, such as Anonymous, *Jóvenes sin Futuro* (Youth without a Future), *No Les Votes* (Don't Vote for Them), and *Estado de Malestar* (Badfare State).

15. The most active and organized group among older people is known as *yayoflautas*, and given their advanced age, their activism has had high notoriety in the media.

16. In the sociological barometers from the Spanish Sociological Research Center politicians appear as the third problem

faced by the country. Accessible in: http://www.cis.es/cis/opencm/ES/11_barometros/index.jsp (consulted 3/1/2013)

17. It has been especially relevant in the assemblies that took place at Puerta del Sol Assembly (Madrid's central square and one of the main symbols of the city), where proposals resulting from the various district assemblies of the city were discussed and approved.

18. It is relevant to note that this public participation process would hardly be carried out without the application of specific methodologies. This is a specialized knowledge, and only people with experience in this type of technique have been responsible for introducing and consolidating public assemblies in the Indignados movement (usually people with experience in political activism, with leftist or anarchist ideological orientation). Similarly, we can say that this methodology has served as an educational and training implement for the population who mostly didn't have experience with public assemblies. In that sense, it seems like public deliberation methodologies have been "exported" to the US Occupy Wall Street movement. In both cases, we could think of public assemblies as knowledge transfer and collaboration through mutual learning.

19. The indexes of political trust, trust in government, and perceptions of the economy are calculated by translating the rating scale of respondents' answers with the categories "very good," "good," "fair," "poor," or "very poor" to a single percentage value.

20. It is worth noting that even during the years of the so-called "Spanish economic miracle" – José María Aznar's mandate from 1996 to 2004, and Rodrigo Rato as Minister of Economy – trust indexes show a decreasing tendency. This illustrates that citizens' institutional trust does not rely on the country's macro-economic performance (or not mainly) but on a more complex set of interrelated variables and

sociopolitical processes.

21. It is noteworthy that in the Spanish case, the D'Hondt law is the formula applied to translate votes into seats in the Parliament, favoring the most voted-for parties, and thus not favoring the less voted-for parties. While it was considered a good way to strengthen institutional stability right after the transition to democracy in the late 1970s and in the 1980s, almost 40 years later it is highly criticized, and a demand for its change has been made by the Indignados movement.

22. In the case of Spain, unlike other central and north European countries, society has interpreted that alternatives are not right-wing, xenophobic parties, or anti-Europe, at least for the moment, but political parties with different but not extremist political proposals: the Communist Party and UPyD, who have taken advantage of the current crisis of bipartisanship, gaining a relevant position in the political scene. In the recently held elections for the European Parliament, overall one out of four votes were for extreme right parties and/or anti-Europeanist.

23. With Rajoy's Government some corruption affairs coming to light created great social scandal, such as the possible illegal financing of the Partido Popular, or corruption linked to the Royal Family, as well as multiple cases of corruption in the municipal and regional governments across the country. Traditionally, in not a few Spanish towns, mayors were re-elected despite ongoing judicial investigations for alleged corruption. The behavior of politicians, or mostly the election of representatives, is a reflection of society, and the culture of corruption is, with different degrees of intensity, present in all social layers. In times of economic crisis and high unemployment, the population is much less tolerant of political corruption.

24. Issues such as the economic crisis, its causes, consequences, and solutions, the responsibility of politicians and political

parties, the financial sector and the way it functions, the global economy as well as issues of national scope, or the responsibilities of citizens (with the question of whether the population has lived beyond their means) soon came to be discussed for hours and hours in the halls of households through television, pages in the press, and of course the Internet. From one day to another, people wanted to know what was happening, how the world and the economy work, and certainly citizens came to acquire more information and knowledge than before the rise of the movement, and most importantly, to have an interest in and concern for public issues.

25. A small achievement to highlight is the change of the aforementioned Mortgage Law, which takes place just when suicides of people losing their homes occur. While evictions are put into effect punctually, they do not occur in a massive way. However, they do take place with high media coverage and high social impact. Note that this change in law has been widely criticized since it addresses a very small group of people - those assumed to be in a more delicate situation of social exclusion, thus it is seen as a purely cosmetic change.

26. This is what Bourdieu calls "the left hand of the state," in which women play a foremost part. Thought it is not a central part of this book, we can pose as hypotheses the special relevance women are having overall in these protests, and its gender-analytical side. Women are one of the social groups most affected by the economic crisis and the austerity measures, not just considering the just-mentioned protest of movements, but for example measures such as cuts in the public financial aids to dependency (women are mostly the ones in charge of the elderly or disabled), or in pensions for retirement (there is a higher percentage of elderly women than men).

27. See locations in the map: https://www.google.com/maps/s?

msid=21682119947711413034 7.00047e05cbd4ac3d080be&ms
a=0&ll=41.14557,1.713867&spn=10.502047,19.907227

28. Source: Centro de Investigaciones Sociológicas (CIS), Research #3028 – May–June 2014.

29. Source: Centro de Investigaciones Sociológicas (CIS), Research #3033 – July 2014.

30. At this moment IU concurs by on its own to the 20-D general elections under the Ahora en Común label and with barely any representation or financial resources. According to the CIS's regular surveys on voting intentions, in April and July 2015, 37.4% and 45.8% of IU voters do respectively manifest their intention of shifting their vote to Podemos for the next general election, an enormous transfer of votes in just three months.

31. Close examples are Greece and Italy, but with different genesis and outcomes to the Spanish case. In Greece, protesters reached their political representation in the institutional framework with Syriza, a formal, structured, and historic party. In Italy, the most notorious experience is Beppe Grillo and the Five Stars Movement, in the mid-term showing low constancy and being a staging/occasional/ fugitive/reactive option rather than proactive.

32. In the May 2015 local elections Manuela Carmena (Ahora Madrid) and Ada Colau (Barcelona en Comú) have been elected as the city mayors of Madrid and Barcelona respectively, while in the city of Valencia (the third largest city in the country) and its region Mónica Oltra (Compromís) is the main reference leading social and democratic change.

Index

Index

Zero Books

CULTURE, SOCIETY & POLITICS

Contemporary culture has eliminated the concept and public figure of the intellectual. A cretinous anti-intellectualism presides, cheer-led by hacks in the pay of multinational corporations who reassure their bored readers that there is no need to rouse themselves from their stupor. Zer0 Books knows that another kind of discourse – intellectual without being academic, popular without being populist – is not only possible: it is already flourishing. Zer0 is convinced that in the unthinking, blandly consensual culture in which we live, critical and engaged theoretical reflection is more important than ever before.

If you have enjoyed this book, why not tell other readers by posting a review on your preferred book site.

Recent bestsellers from Zero Books are:

In the Dust of This Planet
Horror of Philosophy vol. 1
Eugene Thacker
In the first of a series of three books on the Horror of
Philosophy, *In the Dust of This Planet* offers the genre of horror
as a way of thinking about the unthinkable.
Paperback: 978-1-84694-676-9 ebook: 978-1-78099-010-1

Capitalist Realism
Is there no alternative?
Mark Fisher
An analysis of the ways in which capitalism has presented itself
as the only realistic political-economic system.
Paperback: 978-1-84694-317-1 ebook: 978-1-78099-734-6

Rebel Rebel
Chris O'Leary
David Bowie: every single song. Everything you want to know,
everything you didn't know.
Paperback: 978-1-78099-244-0 ebook: 978-1-78099-713-1

Cartographies of the Absolute
Alberto Toscano, Jeff Kinkle
An aesthetics of the economy for the twenty-first century.
Paperback: 978-1-78099-275-4 ebook: 978-1-78279-973-3

Malign Velocities
Accelerationism and Capitalism
Benjamin Noys
Long listed for the Bread and Roses Prize 2015, *Malign Velocities* argues against the need for speed, tracking acceleration as the symptom of the ongoing crises of capitalism.
Paperback: 978-1-78279-300-7 ebook: 978-1-78279-299-4

Meat Market
Female flesh under Capitalism
Laurie Penny
A feminist dissection of women's bodies as the fleshy fulcrum of capitalist cannibalism, whereby women are both consumers and consumed.
Paperback: 978-1-84694-521-2 ebook: 978-1-84694-782-7

Poor but Sexy
Culture Clashes in Europe East and West
Agata Pyzik
How the East stayed East and the West stayed West.
Paperback: 978-1-78099-394-2 ebook: 978-1-78099-395-9

Romeo and Juliet in Palestine
Teaching Under Occupation
Tom Sperlinger
Life in the West Bank, the nature of pedagogy and the role of a university under occupation.
Paperback: 978-1-78279-637-4 ebook: 978-1-78279-636-7